This
Moment

How to Live Fully and Freely in the Present
Moment

By Matt Valentine

To my wife,
for believing in me,
To my children,
for giving me a sense of purpose,
And to you,
for inspiring me through your courage to walk the journey
to yourself.

"Ceasing to do evil,
Cultivating the good,
Purifying the heart:
This is the teaching of the Buddhas."

- The Buddha

Table of Contents

Preface

That's all any of us ever want out of our lives, no matter what our efforts look like on the outside.

For as long as I can remember, I had the idea in my mind that I was supposed to do something special. Even as a young child I have a few faint memories of thinking, "I'm special. I'm going to do something significant."

Years later, I'd realize that there wasn't really anything special at all about that thought, because we all have it at one point or another. We all believe we're supposed to do something "big" with our lives, that we're special. Little did I know at the time, but that initial idea which was sparked in my mind would lead me all the way down the path I travel today.

For the past six years, I've studied feverishly with one goal in mind. Everything from books like *Think & Grow Rich*, *The Millionaire Mind*, and *The Secret* to John Maxwell's *21 Irrefutable Laws of Leadership*, all books very popular in sales and commission-based business environments due to the focus around self-actualization, or realizing one's potential, and money (a part of self-actualization, to most). I've read just about every major self-development book you can name, from Tony Robbins' *Unlimited Power* to *The Magic of Thinking Big*. Later, I'd dive into Positive Psychology and the study of happiness and our overall well-being by reading the likes of Martin Seligman, Shawn Achor, Sonja Lyubomirsky, and others. Lastly, I moved on to

This Moment

everything spirituality and worldly wisdom, eventually landing on Buddhism, most specifically Zen and the likes of Thich Nhat Hanh, Alan Watts, D.T. Suzuki, Shunryu Suzuki, and other teachers from The Dalai Lama and Pema Chodron to Chogyam Trungpa, and of course, the Buddha.

Each new book I read, each new talk I listened to, and each new person I studied, from the self-actualization arena, to pure "self-development", to "well-being", to "spirituality", I got a little bit closer. But a little bit closer to what? It was always about fulfilling the need, filling the hole I felt inside of myself. Whether it was monetary-based fulfillment, self-actualization, the happiness-based version of self-actualization (which is really what Martin Seligman's *Flourish* was), or some deeper aim to fulfill something within me through spiritual practice, it was all the same one effort...

To realize freedom.

It was freedom, or peace (two sides of the same coin), which is what I was really after. Freedom from the conditions and habitual patterns which held me back and kept me from enjoying what was in front of me all along: *this moment.* It took years before I realized that true freedom is what we're all after from the very start. It just takes many different shapes, each "stage", if you will, becoming a little clearer and more accurately defined, and each stage bringing a little more peace and happiness.

If I was to pinpoint the origin of *This Moment*, that would be it. That is, the path to realizing that we're *all* after the same thing. We all want to realize freedom, we all want to discover true peace and happiness by coming to a place where we can live fully and freely in this moment of our life as it is. That's all any of us ever want out of our lives, no matter what our efforts look like on the outside. But most of us lack clarity and this lack of clarity misguides us to pursuits such as the collection of wealth, fame, and power in an attempt to fill the void we feel in our hearts. But none of these things will ever

This Moment

fill us up, and until we realize this we'll never become truly fulfilled and at peace.

You see, despite all my effort to "become my best self" as I used to refer to it, I was still intensely stressed, anxious, and unhappy. At the time in my life when it was worst, I was about to be a father and was already having enough trouble paying my bills and figuring out what I was going to do with my life. How could I properly raise my son with these challenges in front of me? And with no resolution in sight? It was at that point in which I stopped looking on the surface and began to dig deeper.

I had finally realized after so long that I really had no idea what I was doing. My search for success and my efforts towards realizing my potential had led me nowhere but to more unrest and unhappiness. I began to look at my original quest for self-actualization in another light. It wasn't about being special or doing something special, success or realizing my potential, it was about being free and at peace. Peace and freedom were what I was after all along, I just didn't know it. I didn't have the clarity necessary to see that and so all of my efforts were misguided and only caused me more suffering. This is so often the case for so many people.

From that point on, everything I studied was about the mind, happiness, peace, fulfillment, meaning, and really "figuring things out". It was at that point that I began feeling a little like the Buddha, attempting to find an answer to the suffering I and others were experiencing. Looking back, I see that many of us follow that same path. Some, the lucky ones, realize something is amiss and turn inwards, perhaps intuitively (if you're reading this book, you're on that path whether you realize it or not). We become fed up with our life as it is, and see clearly that what we thought was "it" just isn't working. It's from there that we begin to search from within for the real answer to *the question*. That is, the question of how to transcend our suffering and realize true freedom, the one and only ingredient necessary for true peace and happiness to arise.

Fast-forward to three years ago, I had begun organizing my notes and research (which was mountainous, at that point) into Evernote with regards to everything that I had studied and the ideas which I had developed. What I had discovered, particularly through the practice of Zen, meditation, and mindfulness, had helped me not just get my daily life in order, I had altogether transformed my relationship with my stress and anxiety and brought a great sense of peace and contentment into my life. I knew what I had discovered could help others, so I began contemplating how I could do that most effectively. It was one year later that I created my personal blog, Buddhaimonia.com.

I knew I didn't have all the answers at that point, but I saw Buddhaimonia both as a platform for offering to others what I had found so far and as a valuable opportunity to start formally organizing and further developing my work on the subject. I knew from my business experience that the best way to learn is to put yourself out there, with others, and to start an open conversation. The internet provided the perfect landscape for doing just that as well as doing it in a way that allowed me to grow it into a resource for others.

Two years later, in the present day, I've grown more through Buddhaimonia than in perhaps the entire rest of my life. Putting yourself out there isn't ever easy, but bringing these ideas front and center so that others can utilize them in their own life as well as to see what works and what doesn't work, what was off the mark and what simply needed to be adjusted, has been invaluable. As my own daily practice of meditation and mindful living deepened, I was able to communicate that to the community and in many ways the community helped me grow and kept me grounded (thank you).

I told you this story for two reasons:

This Moment

1. To show you how *This Moment* came to be.

From this story, you can draw a clear line from the initial search for meaning (wanting to be "special") to the development of that idea to a point where clarity was gained (it's about finding peace and freedom in this moment). That initial idea, the search that followed, and the turning point where I realized my efforts had been misguided all along were key moments on the journey.

Once I had shifted to finding an answer to the real question- not how to fill myself up through success or attaining anything for that matter, but how to live fully and freely in the present moment (in our life as it is), because we were whole all along- I attained a wholesome purpose and from that Buddhaimonia was born. And it's the refined discoveries and development into a teachable practice that Buddhaimonia helped me realize which became *This Moment*.

2. To give you a clear example of how our search for an answer to *the question looks* in real life.

Whether we know it or not, we're all searching for the same thing. Whether you're looking for the one, success, fulfillment through your work, fame, riches, or are following some other path, it's all the same one effort. We're all searching for peace and freedom. Peace and freedom is what we want. But we lack the clarity necessary to see what we truly need (or what truly *is*) and become fixated, through various life conditioning, on false remedies. False answers.

But when you remove the misguided efforts, worrying about the future, regretting the past, and look upon your life *as it is*, what are you left with? You're left simply with *this moment*. It's this moment which is all that's ever been, the

This Moment

present moment. And it's in this moment that we can find peace. It's in this moment where all possibility exists. It's in this moment that we can work to live fully awake to our lives, that we can choose to focus on what really matters and nourish our well-being, that we can work to break through the barriers which hold us back from experiencing life in its fullness, and it's in this moment that we can go beyond the confines of the ego by opening our heart to the world and experience true love.

How do you realize true freedom? How do you truly live life fully and freely? That is *the question*, and it's the question I was trying to find an answer to all my life (whether I knew it or not). Whether it was the desire to feel special, successful, stable, or whole it was always just different shades of the same one effort. But all of those efforts sought to change the reality of my life in the now. I rejected the present moment and sought to change things, much of the time cultivating a sort of resentment for the state of my life as it was, however subtle.

So, my efforts to find an answer all fell in vain because every effort rejected the truth: that this moment is all that's ever been. It's all we have and by denying ourselves this fact we deny ourselves all we've ever truly wanted. But, by accepting this fact and then working to live fully and freely in our life *as it is*, we open ourselves up to the possibility of peace and happiness. Peace and happiness in this moment- the present moment.

This Moment

This Moment

Introduction

...if you make your best effort you can discover a great magic in your life. The magic of allowing yourself to be fully, as you are, in the present moment.

Every day that I sit to write, record, or do whatever else I have to do, I ask myself the question: "What is the best use of my time?" In this context, I'm trying to be the most productive with my time, so that I don't become mindlessly drawn away by less important tasks. But, this same principle can be applied to our entire lives and in a wider sense to live fully in each moment.

In each moment, we're either awake or asleep (and to varying degrees). In the same way, we're either free or bound by our conditioning and ignorance. To live fully in this moment, to be fully engaged in our lives and able to experience the beauty that exists all around us, is to be both mindful and free of this conditioning. To live even a single moment mindfully, fully alive to this moment, and without obstructions, having moved beyond the conditioning that binds us in this life and causes us so much suffering to a place of boundless freedom, is a taste of enlightenment itself.

It's like eating an apple with no sense of taste. One person eats the apple but does not taste it, or at best has a muted sense of taste and barely experiences the flavor of the apple. This is where most of us are at. The more awake person fully tastes the ripe, juicy apple in all its glory. The further awakened one in that moment more fully experiences the beauty of the apple and sees deeply into it.

This Moment

How amazing it is to think that we put so much work into creating delicious dishes and special foods, and still some of the most delicious of all foods is the fruit which grows on its own completely away from the hands of the human production process. Perfect just as they are, they exist as a testament that we can find everything we need in the natural world. So, the awakened one eats the same apple, but they experience the full reality of the apple. We *all* taste the apple, because the apple is life, but our ability to freely experience the fullness of reality- this moment- differs.

So, then the question is, how can we bring ourselves to that place? How can we truly live fully and freely in the present moment? To live fully and freely in this moment is to live our best life. It means to live fully awake, able to experience the beauty that exists all around us as well as to be fully liberated, free from the conditioning which binds us and causes us so much suffering. Answering that question, and then living it, is the single most worthwhile effort of all.

That is the question which *This Moment* intends to answer. It's a big topic, without a doubt, one which if fully covered could sprawl a 500+ page tome and still not be done exploring every facet of it. And yet, at the same time, one sentence can explain everything that you need to hear. My hope is that with *This Moment*, you're supplied with everything that's essential to set out on your journey of living fully alive and freely within this moment. It's a life-long endeavor, but if you make your best effort you can discover a great magic in your life. The magic of allowing yourself to be fully, as you are, in the present moment.

The 4 Principles

How do we design our lives so that we don't just live more mindfully, but so that we break free from the barriers which obstruct our ability to fully and freely experience the

This Moment

incredible beauty and peace of the present moment? And how do we put ourselves in a position so that we can experience that on an everyday basis? The basic ingredients of *This Moment*- the four principles- are about doing just that.

It might sound nice, to speak about living fully and freely in the present moment, to open ourselves fully to our life as it is and be simply at peace in this moment- whatever we may be presented with. But, what exactly does that even mean? And, more importantly, how do we actually begin to make that a reality? *This Moment* isn't a simply poetic piece of difficult to decipher advice and cryptic language. My work, from the moment I began my research, practice, and experimentation, has always been to distill things down to their essence. Then, to transmit that in a simple, straightforward, and practical way. And that's what I seek to do in *This Moment*.

The book is separated into four major parts. These four parts are the four major principles of the book and together form a complete idea as well as outline a complete practice. Each Part, and the subsequent chapters, deals with either important foundational principles of the practice or major roadblocks which inhibit our ability to live fully and freely in the present moment, both together providing the blueprint for designing a more peaceful and meaningful life. Each principle has a lot to it, but at the same time is broken down in a simple way and with practical instructions for living that particular principle more wisely in your daily life. The four principles are:

1. Living mindfully
2. Living simply
3. Living naturally
4. Living lovingly

Before we get started, it's important that we delve into the four principles so that you have a clear understanding of how each contributes to the overall aim of the book:

Living Mindfully

In *Part I, Living Mindfully*, you'll learn everything you need to know about bringing mindfulness into your life. We'll talk about the basics, why mindfulness is so important, and the most important things to keep in mind in mindfulness practice. We'll also cover the foundational practices, a game plan for actually changing your "set point" (or habit energy) from mindless to more often mindful, and one of the most important subjects of all: how to make friends with yourself by walking the path of mindfulness.

To live mindfully is indeed the foundation of *This Moment*. It's mindfulness which provides the fertilizer for us to not only gain the calmness and clarity of mind necessary to work through our difficult challenges, but to also further nourish our well-being in any given moment. It's mindfulness which allows us to calm the mind and heal the effects of stress and anxiety. It's also mindfulness which allows us to gain great clarity, which leads to important insights that change the way we see the world, and consequently how we live.

Having heard all of that, you might be thinking, "what else is really necessary?" And, indeed, many in the West who have adopted the practice of mindfulness in recent years have taken it as a sort of "panacea" of sorts. But, Buddhist wisdom tells us otherwise. Mindfulness is simply one part in the equation for total peace of mind. Without the other three principles in *This Moment*, our practice would be left lacking important tools for working through the greater issues in our life, such as the distractions caused by the modern lifestyle, the habitual patterns we've had for years which are wholly unfamiliar with this new way of life- of slowing down, of paying attention, and of being mindful- and of which fight back voraciously, the relentless attacks of the inner dialogue, and working through difficult principles such as impermanence and the "void of the heart", among other things.

So, while *Living Mindfully* is the foundation, to call the other three principles supporting members would be to severely understate their importance. In fact, each principle could be considered of equal importance in many ways (and depending on the spiritual tradition you've grown up in, *Living Lovingly* could alternatively be considered the foundational principle). With even one of these four principles taken away, the entire path breaks down. Or, at the very least, is much, much more difficult to walk.

Living Intentionally

Part II, Living Intentionally, is about intentionally living your life in a way that is conducive to greater peace and happiness. In *Living Intentionally*, we talk about the overall environment of your daily life: your goals, your priorities (focus), what you consume both mentally and physically, the qualities you give and don't give attention to, designing a strong and healthy daily practice, and how you live and approach that daily practice.

Living Intentionally is part simplifying your life to remove distractions and allow you more time to focus on what's most important, part mindful consumption to make sure you're watering more wholesome seeds in your life than unwholesome ones, part identifying your priorities and shifting your focus to promote your well-being, and part purifying the quality of your day-to-day effort to keep your practice strong, effective, easeful, and enjoyable.

Part II largely supports the other three principles, especially your effort to live more mindfully. Without *Living*

Intentionally, you're likely to be lacking focus with little chance of making mindfulness, or any practice in the book, a way of life, living in a way that you water unwholesome seeds that harm your well-being, living and working in a way that you prioritize mindlessness over mindfulness, and complicating your mind and life with too much busyness and not enough taking care of yourself.

It's hard to imagine the book without *Part II*, because while it doesn't revolve around any particularly significant spiritual principle, it's something which is prioritized in every spiritual tradition in the world. And that's *an environment that is conducive to the cultivation of those spiritual, or nourishing, principles.* A clear example of *Living Intentionally* in action is that of monastic living. What other reason is there for the monastic lifestyle but to afford the ability to focus in on one's spiritual practice? That's the entire point and it's something which *Part II* seeks to replicate within the confines of a more typical modern lifestyle.

Living Naturally

The idea behind *This Moment* is simple: to identify, and outline, a simple, straightforward, and reliable path for living more fully and freely as well as more skillfully amid our challenges in each moment of our life. But it's not so easy to live life fully and freely in each moment. Many things can get in our way.

Part III, Living Naturally, is about overcoming major challenges. It's part helping you overcome common challenges, such as stress and anxiety, but more importantly it's about helping you work through the larger and more significant challenges we experience in our lives: the fact of our own impermanence, the difficulty in expressing ourselves honestly, when (and how) to let go, and the various ways we create friction in our lives, especially through attachment and aversion.

The reality is, we never get away from challenge. It's a part of our lives and there's really nothing we can do about it. A life filled with rainbows and unicorns and zero adversity of any kind is just a fantasy. But, that doesn't mean we're bound to experience pain and suffering for the rest of our lives. Adversity may be a part of our life forever in some form, but we can change how we *relate* to that adversity with mindfulness and meditative practice and principles such as compassion and loving-kindness. By changing how we relate to our challenges, we completely change how they affect us. And by changing how they affect us, through skillful action, we have the ability to radically transform our lives and remove much of that pain and suffering.

The practice of mindful & intentional living, as well as the practice of loving-kindness, all help us work through these various challenges. But simply saying, "practice mindfulness and you'll overcome this challenge", isn't enough. *Part III* talks specifically about a number of the most significant challenges we're faced with in our lives and walks you through the path and practice of more skillfully handling each in everyday practical terms. There's no easy way out, if a way out exists at all, for any of these challenges, but there is a more skillful path which leads to less pain and suffering and more more peace and happiness in day-to-day life, and that's what *Part III, Living Naturally,* is about.

Living Lovingly

Mindfulness has spread throughout the Western world in the past decade and this is a very good thing. This is the natural part of the process of an awakening people, as the world has seen many times before. But, as we begin to learn more about mindfulness and meditation practice in the West, and as accompanying fields of psychology and scientific research as well as a general interest in techniques and solutions to promote our mental well-being develop, we will see emphasis on more than just mindfulness and meditation in general, although that will stay an important aspect, if not the foundation. Even now, we've begun to see great results from scientific studies on the practice of loving-kindness and once again are drawing parallels between Buddhist wisdom and modern scientific research findings.

Part IV, Living Lovingly, and the final principle of This Moment, is about living with true love. True love in the Buddhist sense of living and loving with equanimity (or in a free and open way that doesn't clip our loved one's wings- or our own), with a sympathetic joy and the ability to delight in other's good fortune, with compassion and the desire to relieve the suffering of others, and finally with loving-kindness, often described as a kind of love defined by acts of kindness and caring.

For those wondering primarily what This Moment will do for you, as many understandably will be, you might be wondering what the Buddhist principle of True Love has to offer you as it all seems to deal with others. The Buddhist principle of True Love isn't confined to romantic love but rather includes (or can include) all beings. That includes yourself. Without a doubt, we love ourselves just as we love others.

...We love ourselves in either a free and open way, or in a confining and critical way.

...We love ourselves in either a joyous way, rejoicing in our good fortune and successes, or constantly beating ourselves up and always telling ourselves we're not good enough.

...We love ourselves in either a compassionate way, taking care of ourselves when we experience some pain or suffering, or a neglectful way, ignoring our needs and never really doing what's necessary to take care of ourselves.

...and we love ourselves in either a kind way, being kind to ourselves when we suffer a setback, failure, internal or external criticism, or suffering of any kind, or in an unkind way, always talking down to ourselves and making ourselves suffer more due to our own actions against ourselves.

True love, and the quality of love we have for ourselves, plays a significant part in our overall well-being and there's so many different ways that it manifests in our daily lives. The quality of loving-kindness is a perfect companion to mindfulness and is often inseparable from it when working through challenges.

In *Part IV, Living Lovingly*, you'll learn more about true love and how love plays a part in our search for meaning in life (and how to avoid falling into the trap of dependent love). You'll also learn how to walk the path of love in your daily life, how the way you interact with loved ones can be a mirror for your viewing your own challenges and unskillfulness, how to live with true love and cultivate loving-kindness through various different formal and informal meditative practices, along with a final word about taking what you've learned and changing the world through your daily actions and the cultivation of Great Compassion.

There was a part of me that consistently felt the title *This Moment* and the subtitled *How to Live Fully and Freely in the Present Moment* were too simple. I felt that I was possibly oversimplifying the point and principles of the book. But, the more I thought about it the more I realized that it's not too simple. It's just right.

This Moment is about the most important thing in life. And that's the very quality of life itself for us- how we experience life. Or, in other words, whether we're stressed, anxious and discontent or happy, free and at peace.

...You could say that it's a book about spiritual practice. And it is, but that's incorrect because to separate "spiritual" from "everyday life" is a gross misunderstanding.

...You could say that it's a book about peace and happiness. And it is, but that's incorrect because separating peace and happiness from the rest of your life- the challenges and adversity- is a gross misunderstanding.

...And you could say that it's a book about overcoming challenges and realizing freedom, and it is, but that's incorrect because that's the purpose of spiritual practice and the pursuit of peace and happiness in the first place, so to separate any of those from one another is a gross misunderstanding.

So I came to see that *This Moment*, and it's accompanying subtitle of *How to Life Fully and Freely in the Present Moment*, were in fact perfectly fitting. That *is* what it's all about- to live more fully, realizing that you were whole all along and never really needed anything to fill yourself up. And to live more freely, free from the chains of habit and conditioning which bind us and cause us to suffer in so many different ways.

Keep in mind, though, that the most important piece of all is always the quality of your own effort. The words on this page are useful for nothing more than giving you a guide by which you can more skillfully live your day-to-day life. But, if you don't follow the practice, if you don't strive to live more mindfully, more intentionally, more naturally, or more lovingly, than nothing will happen. For actually changing your life, this book is no better than a table cover. Words on a page will never stand up and breathe for you, walk for you, think, or act for you. It's you who needs to take action. It's you who is always the most important principle of all.

For those ready to live the practice of peace, to bring the four principles alive in your everyday life, I want you to know that we walk together on this path. You're never alone,

This Moment

never travelling without a partner to lean on. When the going gets tough, all you have to do is take a moment to breathe and imagine me sitting with you, walking with you. This is available to you in each and every moment. I wish you the best of luck on your journey ahead and hope that *This Moment* serves as a worthy and loving companion.

Peace,
Matt

This Moment

Part I: Living Mindfully

This Moment

Mindfulness: The Ground of Peace

There is no other place, and no other way, we'll discover peace and stability than through discarding all false notions and realizing how firmly rooted we are to the present moment.

Years ago, I bought a book on a whim. Little did I know that it would completely transform my life and lead me on the path I tread today. That book was *The Miracle of Mindfulness*, and it was the first book that truly taught me about the power of mindfulness. The book is technically a letter written by author Thich Nhat Hanh to a friend in Vietnam at the time, so it's not organized particularly well nor does it clearly explain everything it mentions. But, it's a beautifully profound book written by someone I consider a dear teacher. It was more than enough.

At the time, I could barely get my head out of the future long enough to get my work done and handle all my other responsibilities. I was stressed out about my bills, worrying about the future and how I was going to support my future son (who was to be born just months from then), and constantly reflected on the disappointment I felt towards myself for having still not accomplished anything of real value in my life.

It's hard, perhaps impossible, to completely put into words what mindfulness did for me. When I think of how mindfulness changed my life all I want to do is silently scream from a mountain top, where no one will hear me but the rocks and clouds. When I think of how profound discovering, and practicing, mindfulness has been for me I feel a sense of heaviness in reflecting on so many difficult memories, now with a sense of peace, relief, and sincere joy.

Why Mindfulness?

So, why mindfulness? I mean, exactly why is it so profound? Why is it the foundation of this "practice of peace" I've spoken of since the Introduction? How can one thing really be so important? Explaining why it's the foundation of this daily practice is easy, but explaining all the reasons why mindfulness is so profound can be quite difficult. Let's start with why, fundamentally, mindfulness is the foundation.

Consider your eyesight for a moment. Now, you may or may not have perfect eyesight. Assuming you wear glasses or contact lenses, all of us see at least "good enough" to manage through our everyday lives without any hassle. But, imagine if your eyesight suddenly wasn't so good, or eyesight quality aids suddenly no longer existed. What would it be like to try and navigate everyday life with sketchy eyesight? It would be incredibly difficult and stressful, if not impossible. Imagine getting up in the morning, getting out of bed, going to the restroom, putting your clothes on, walking to the kitchen, and preparing breakfast. All without eyesight sharp enough to tell if you're looking at a glass of water or a bottle of bleach.

Now, imagine walking outside, getting in your car, and having to drive to work half-way blind. Now, imagine having to get your job done, every single day. Then, having to drive home, cook dinner over a hot stove (or drive through a narrow drive-thru, your choice), take a shower, and get ready for bed. Finally, turning off the lights and going to bed. If only others could experience what it's like to live in darkness, you say to yourself as you fall asleep, then everyone would know what it's like to live like I do.

But of course, in real life, you couldn't say this to yourself, because you'd have no idea you couldn't see. That's because this darkness is mindlessness, the lack of "mind sight" necessary with which to view ourselves and our inner workings with clarity. And this mindlessness, unlike bad eyesight, isn't noticeable unless you've experienced the latter-*mindfulness*.

It's mindfulness which allows us to wake up to ourselves, to wake up to our lives and what goes on in our mind on a moment-to-moment basis. This leads to numerous significant events which are critical to our overall mental well-being. Mindfulness is like 20/20 vision for your mind. You see things you never noticed before. What was once blurry and unrecognizable now becomes clear and identifiable. Without this sharp level of vision, you'd lack the clarity necessary to navigate life's challenges and develop the skillfulness to manage them and properly nourish yourself, leading to greater peace and happiness in daily life. But more than just a keen awareness, mindfulness is also the practice of keeping ourselves present to this moment, because you can only stay focused on one point for so long before your concentration falters. This is a critical factor in our ability to stay present.

So then, we know why mindfulness is the foundation of living fully and freely in the present moment, but what exactly does practicing and living with mindfulness do? Or more specifically, how does it help us more skillfully navigate life's challenges and cultivate greater peace and happiness?

1. Mindfulness helps you identify patterns

I talk often about how mindfulness helps us better navigate internal challenges. One way this is clearly demonstrated is in it's ability to help us identify patterns.

What do I mean by identifying patterns? Mindfulness, more than anything else, gives us clarity. When we begin to gain clarity, we start to be able to identify bad patterns of behavior such as avoidance when faced with stress and difficult situations, bias or attitude in the face of a certain person or persons, and a bad habit when handling a specific strong emotion such as fear or anger.

When we work to identify these patterns and then handle them skillfully, our whole world can change. Suddenly, we see clearly all the various ways we suffer and, in many cases, the simple (but not necessarily easy) solutions to overcoming, or at least better managing, these bad patterns of behavior.

2. Mindfulness shows you clearly the source of the problem (and gives you a way to overcome, or better work with, it)

More than just identifying patterns, with practice mindfulness can show you clearly where the source of the problem exists altogether. If you notice you mentally judge a specific person every time you walk up to them, with practice you may realize that you have a bottled-down sense of envy and jealousy towards them because you feel inadequate having still not achieved any of your own goals and dreams in life. And that's just one of countless examples.

But, you're not just left alone at this point to figure out how to overcome it. Many internal challenges can be overcome by your compassionate and loving presence alone, needing nothing more than for you to stop and breathe mindfully and to send loving-kindness and compassion to yourself until the challenge can dissipate having now risen to the surface of your consciousness. We'll talk about exercises for cultivating the qualities of loving-kindness and compassion in Part IV.

3. Mindfulness gives you a way to bring yourself back to "center" 24/7

Mindfulness isn't restricted to the meditation cushion, although sitting in meditation is the foundation of mindfulness practice. Mindfulness is a tool you can use anywhere and anytime you feel overwhelmed, stressed, anxious, fearful, or angry. For me, sometimes this was going back to my breath. Other times, this was walking mindfully or simply stopping and being mindful of the feeling or emotion. In every case, this was about going home to myself and nourishing my well-being simply and compassionately with my total presence.

The simple act of stopping and becoming present to ourselves from time to time is often all that's necessary to keep the "crazy" out of our lives. Of course, much more is necessary for us to truly find some semblance of peace of mind, but this powerful act of stopping or simply becoming mindful of what we're doing as we go about our day is highly nourishing and beneficial. In this section, Part I, we'll cover numerous mindfulness practices, such as the ones I just mentioned, for allowing you to bring yourself back to center.

4. Mindfulness shows you the truth of the present moment

My mindfulness practice showed me that the past and future are nothing more than ideas in our mind. Sure, the past happened and it may be important, but it doesn't literally exist anywhere but in the mind. And the future, while important to plan for and consider, in actual practice is nothing more than estimations, assumptions, and imagination. We live tied to the realms of past and future as much as the present, to the point where we believe that they're real, and in doing so we suffer. Understanding this changed how I live my life.

There is no other place, and no other way, we'll discover peace and stability than through discarding all false notions and realizing how firmly rooted we are to the present moment. So much of the chaos that exists in our mind comes from regretting and reflecting about the past, worrying about and building up the future, and imagining all kinds of possibilities in between. This thinking will never completely cease, but the problem is we get so caught up in it thinking we're off somewhere else, when the only place we ever really are- even when we're thinking- is in the present moment.

On top of that, it's the resisting of the present moment that causes so much pain and confusion for us as well. When something happens, we often fight it, and so by resisting the present reality we cause friction to ourselves and our life at large. Mindfulness will fully reunite you with the present moment and show you the peace and freedom that exists within it. This is a lesson no one should live without.

5. Mindfulness shows you the path to true happiness

As I mentioned in the Introduction, most of us chase happiness thinking if we make a lot of money, find our dream partner, or attain great power we'll be set for life. The insights I received from my mindfulness practice not only simplified life and showed me that everyone is searching for happiness, just in countless different ways, but that true happiness (or at least, what we *call* happiness) is found in inner peace and freedom.

In a state of inner peace, we still feel but are less unearthed by life's difficult challenges and maintain a clear and ever-present calmness throughout life. And when we're not facing down challenges, we're able to clearly identify moments of peace and joy and appreciate all that's around us, even something as simple as the beauty of the blue sky (even sometimes *during* these challenges). You don't know it from the outside, but when you begin to practice you realize that these simple moments are absolutely and totally fulfilling. They're the single most profound moments of your life and they allow you to feel utterly at peace with everything around you.

Of course, realizing true inner peace is easier said than done, but gaining clarity about the path and seeing clearly how we get there is a huge step in the right direction. And mindfulness not only helps us do that but it continues to be our guide along the path.

6. Mindfulness shows you that we're all interconnected

The fact that we're all intrinsically connected isn't some fluffy principle which sounds nice, it's something which you can experience right now in your daily life. But, the way we usually live our lives our awareness is hovering right below the signs so to speak. So we rarely, if ever, see it. Once you begin practicing mindfulness and living with greater awareness in the present, you'll begin to see the natural rhythm of life and how we all depend on so many different things just to come to be as we are in the present and to continue on living each day.

This isn't limited to people either. This includes all other living and non-living things- on land, in the ocean, and in the sky. This can be seen in very concrete ways- in the way we depend on the coral reefs or on the delivery of our local food and water supply for instance- but also in a much deeper way. In a very real way, we exist in the clouds, in the rain and in the mountains. And they in us.

This single realization can change the way you live your entire life. From the way you treat others, to what you devote your time to, the products you consume, and the causes you support.

7. Mindfulness shows you how to appreciate life

Beyond that, you'll realize that we're not just interconnected, but that this world is downright crazy. What I mean by that is, have you ever thought about the amount of work the world at large had to put in to delivering all of the products that exist in your home to you as they are?

From your soap, to your shampoo, to your razor, to your shoes, your clothes, coffee or tea, each item on your breakfast plate, your stove, refrigerator, computer, and everything in between. Your mindfulness practice will allow you to begin seeing things much differently than you once did. Think about the amount of people, the amount of machines, the amount of worldly resources, and the thousands of hours of time it took to create and further manage and develop this elaborate system of living we've developed for ourselves.

This is the world you live in every day, and realizing this, through mindfulness practice, can become a source of great fascination, joy, and appreciation. Always perfectly at balance, yet unbelievably complicated and seemingly fragile on the surface, once you realize this the world is revealed as being both unbelievably fascinating and awe-inspiring.

8. Mindfulness shows you that the present moment is a renewable source of joy

We can find some measure of happiness in memories, in recollecting about positive experiences, and therefore feeling better about our lives. But, this form of happiness isn't possible for everyone, and as we go about our lives past experiences take on new meaning, so this doesn't necessarily last forever nor is it a dependable source of happiness. That's on top of the fact that these memories always have to fight against the present state of our lives, so they don't always have the same effect.

Experiential happiness- that is, living in the present moment and experiencing all the little joys life has to offer (which are really significant when looked at closely with mindfulness)- is a renewable source of happiness that can never be taken from us. This is where true happiness exists. By practicing mindfulness, and becoming better attuned to the beautiful little intricacies of life, you begin to cultivate a great sense of joy in your daily life. And this can never be taken from you, no matter what's going on in the rest of your life.

9. Mindfulness shows you that life doesn't have to be lived on fast-forward

Ancient India was believed to have a much different outlook on time than we do now. In the East, their view of time was believed to be more cyclic than linear like it's always been in the West (and is throughout the entire world today). By that I mean the belief was that the same general cycle of occurrences happened over and over repeatedly. This view likely arose from their understanding of how we live our lives more than anything.

When looked at more closely, this cyclic view of time really is the way we live- always going through the motions, repeating the same cycle of pain and suffering, joy and happiness, then pain and suffering again usually without end or until we realize some level of greater awakening through meditative practice. This view of time is very wise and very helpful as it draws attention to this cycle of suffering. The modern interpretation of time on the other hand, believed to have been born from Judaism, is linear. This means that time is a straight line extending out indefinitely, no period of time every overlapping with another.

What does all of this mean, and why does it matter? It's because of this linear view of time that we rush around so much. We believe we need to make the most of every single second of our lives for fear of wasting time. In this view, time is a limited resource. This forces us to rush around all day long trying not to waste a single minute of life. Which, ironically, keeps us from ever really living. What's far more important than time, no matter what your view, is to be fully present to this moment and attending to your life right now as it is, as opposed to always thinking about later today, tomorrow, or

This Moment

next week. Some of this is necessary, but when you're always living in this way you're trying to catch something which can never be found and you end up spending your entire life unhappy and unfulfilled. When you practice mindfulness, you begin to realize that slowing down isn't just nice, but that a slower pace of life is our natural way and most conducive to our health and happiness.

Being Fully of this Moment

"Treat every moment as your last. It is not preparation for something else."

- Shunryu Suzuki

       So far, we've talked about the *why*- why mindfulness is the foundation of the practice outlined in *This Moment* and ultimately why it's so important overall. Now, we turn to the *how*. To be more precise, the remainder of Part I touches on varying degrees of how, from what to do moment-to-moment while practicing, to how to do individual practices, to how to make mindfulness a way of life, to how to navigate the journey to yourself with mindfulness as a whole. In this chapter, we'll discuss the moment-to-moment aspect of mindfulness. That is, how to approach the practice of mindfulness- and really how to live- with all of your being and in each moment. But, first, it's important that we establish a working definition of mindfulness for those not completely familiar with the term. Here it is:

Mindfulness is a specific kind of moment-to-moment awareness of present events. It's the capacity to be, and keep, ourselves attentive to this moment, typically while centering our attention on one point in an effort to anchor ourselves more effectively to the present moment.

Given the fact that I write and teach about mindfulness and meditative practice, I've found myself having to express a definition of mindfulness on a number of occasions, each time refining that definition both for clarity of understanding the *quality* of mindfulness and also for comprehension of what the actual *practice* of mindfulness looks like in the moment. In my last book, *Zen for Everyday Life*, I actually separated those definitions in hopes of providing a second working definition that would help others adopt the practice more easily, instead of just learning about it from an intellectual standpoint. Looking back, it was very helpful, but I also see that it further complicates things and have decided on a single definition that I feel accurately defines both the quality and practice enough to get someone started. Ultimately, it's not the definition in either case that will help you truly understand mindfulness. Only the practice, and experience, of being mindful itself will do that.

One Thing

This is the first of three principles we'll talk about that complete the mantra for this chapter: "Do one thing, with one mind, in one (this) moment." "Do *one thing*" is exactly what it sounds like: it's single tasking. This is perhaps the simplest lesson in this entire book, but it holds no less importance.

A Zen monk or nun living the monastic way of life goes about their daily life in a way that they're totally and completely focused on the task at hand and a key aspect of that is to simply do one thing at a time- whatever it is that you're doing in that moment. Whatever demands your presence, you're there for it fully.

Multi-tasking has not only been proven to be ineffective, it's actually damaging.[1] Making the commitment to live your life in a way that you do the *one thing* that's most important in each moment means to live with greater clarity and perform more effectively at everything you do. It also promotes greater concentration and mindfulness, the point of this first principle. Of course, there are times in your life where things aren't so black-and-white, sometimes more than one thing will call for your attention and you won't exactly know what to place your undivided attention on. But, the point is to *aim* to do so in every moment, to *give your best effort*. If you give your best effort, it will be enough.

One Mind

To do something with every ounce of your being means to live with mindfulness and concentration in this moment. It means to be totally and completely focused on that one thing with every ounce of yourself. This doesn't just mean to avoid multi-tasking, though, it also means to be totally concentrated on the one thing that you're doing in each moment.

You don't open a door while forcefully pushing away any thoughts or outside sounds that arise, you open the door with all of your being, two hands and one mind on the door knob, while still being openly mindful of whatever arises within that moment. Keep in mind that this isn't a hard, vein-popping, concentration that you're acting with. This is a soft but persistent concentration on the present moment (concentration is the constant partner of mindfulness). You're being here, awake to your life, in every moment. And that's really what this is all about. It's about bringing that same single-pointed and mindful awareness that's cultivated in meditation practice from the meditation cushion into your everyday life. And there are surprisingly simple ways to begin cultivating this.

The most important way to begin cultivating this "one mind" attitude is to simply do one thing with all of your *body*. Yes, body. We tend to underestimate just how connected the body and mind really are. By putting your entire body behind an action you send a signal to the mind that you're completely focused on this very task in this moment, and that helps you cultivate this *one mind* attitude. Examples of this are opening a door with both hands, as opposed to with one hand on your smartphone and one hand on the door knob, holding your cup of coffee, tea, or other with both hands, and sitting while maintaining proper posture while working, eating, or doing anything else. Each of these tasks involves you putting your entire body into the task at hand so that you summon your entire mind to it as well.

Nothing special is necessary to begin living your life with *one mind*. Simply make it a point to focus your mind in on the task at hand, through light concentration, bringing yourself back when you notice you've lost your focus, and utilizing the power of the body to influence the mind. If you can do this, you can cultivate the habit of living with *one mind*.

One Moment

To be fully *of* this moment means to give your full being *to this moment*. *This moment* is *one moment*, the only moment there ever is. To live in this way means you leave nothing on the table, reserve no part of yourself, hold nothing back and regret nothing. You act as one unstoppable force in this moment. Shunryu Suzuki, the great Zen master and founder of San Francisco Zen Center, the first Zen center in the U.S., had this to say:

This Moment

You should not have any remains after you do something.
But this does not mean to forget all about it. In order not to
leave any traces, when you do something, you should do it
with your whole body and mind; you should be concentrated
on what you do. You should do it completely, like a good
bonfire.
You should not be a smoky fire. You should burn yourself
completely. If you do not burn yourself completely, a trace of
yourself will be left in what you do.

The way most of us live our lives, we're usually doing
something now in preparation for something later. In each
moment, we're more concentrated on the next moment than
we are *the present moment*. Because of this, we're never fully
present to our lives and almost always living in our heads half
asleep. To live mindfully, deeply, fully engaged in *this moment*
is to let go of the future and be fully of this moment- the
present moment. It doesn't necessarily mean you cease
planning for the future, as some planning is necessary. How
would we ever get anything done if we never planned
anything? So, some degree of planning is necessary, but when
you do your entire mental focus is on the act of planning *in the*
present for the future. The focus should always be on living
fully in the present moment.

The most important things to pay attention to are fear
of the future and aversion to the present. Fear of the future
makes us either focus constantly on planning for the future
and avoiding the present or mindlessly distracting ourselves
and doing neither. Aversion to the present makes us hate
being present and rather constantly planning to improve
things or daydreaming in the future. This can take time as
future moments are always trying to push us along and past
moments are always tugging at us, either bringing us down in
this moment or trying to get us to change the present moment
for the "better". But, with practice, we can begin to more

clearly see when we're acting mindfully and when we're just eating our future plans. And the dedication to living with mindfulness and concentration allows us to do that.

Breath as Life

All you have to do is stop and breathe. It's deceptively simple, but more powerful than can ever be put into words.

When I was younger, I used to play video games for hours on end. I could go what seemed like days straight, getting up only to eat, go to the restroom, for school, and on the rare excursion with friends. During this time, I'd completely lose myself in what I was doing. For hours, I'd completely lose sense of my own body. I played what are considered "open world" type games where I'd adventure to far-off lands and join quests to become stronger and advance along a specified storyline. I *was* the game during those hours, more so than I was ever truly present in real life.

If you've never done this, or something like it, before, then it might seem foreign to you. But, the reality is, we live most of our lives this way. We live going from one moment to the next mindlessly, never truly present to this moment.

But, we have a tool. We don't have to go on living mindlessly from one moment to the next. You now know that mindfulness is the master tool which makes peace, happiness and ultimately freedom possible. It's the very thing which allows us to become fully awake to our lives in the present moment, and, when paired with concentration, allows us to gain great clarity about ourselves. But, we haven't yet discussed exactly how that looks in actual practice.

Breath is the bridge which unites mind and body. It's what allows us to go home to ourselves in the present moment and become fully awake to our lives. And it's the basis for all mindfulness and meditative practice.

The breath is also where life and death meet. Breath is the very symbol of life, and the lack-there-of the most identifiable signifier of the opposite. It interestingly enough holds significance in both Eastern and Western spiritual traditions, the English *spirit* coming from the Latin *spiritus*, meaning "breath".

With the practice of mindful breathing, we can reunite mind and body as one in an instant and bring peace to a clouded mind. All you have to do is stop and breathe. It's deceptively simple, but more powerful than can ever be put into words. And you can breathe mindfully anytime and anywhere. In a moment of free time, a break at work, a quiet minute in the morning before we begin our day, or in a time of hardship when we need to temper a swelling storm within our mind and heart. The practice of mindful breathing is our constant guide and a way to bring ourselves back to center during difficult moments.

Mindful Breathing

The practice of mindful breathing is so important, and so fundamental, that it deserves no less than its own chapter. Breathing is the most commonly used point of concentration across all forms of meditation as well as the most common of all mindfulness practices. Meditation, fundamentally, is the practice of concentrating on an object in the effort to cultivate some quality of mind. It's for this reason that all mindfulness practice, in a way, could be considered meditation. But, typically, the more concentrated practice of mindful breathing, while sitting in a quiet setting and giving ourselves the greatest ability to focus the mind on one point, is considered mindfulness meditation practice.

In the practice of mindfulness, all mindfulness practice, you're very lightly and loosely concentrating on something while being mindful of everything which arises within your field of awareness (think: being fully aware in an open and all-inclusive way). Of course, that sounds nice, but the practice rarely looks so pretty in the beginning. It really looks like this:

1. Focus on the breath →
2. Three seconds later, lose concentration →
3. "Wake up" 2 minutes later ("what happened?"), return to the breath →
4. Three seconds later, lose concentration again →
5. Wake up 1 minute later, return to the breath
6. (repeat)

Just know this is perfectly normal and that, with time, your mind will begin to quiet and become clearer.

How to Practice: Mindful Breathing

Mindful breathing can be done as a form of sitting meditation or just standing in your home, office, outside in nature, or anywhere else and for however long you decide, even just a single breath. There are really no restrictions to the practice, but, it's most often done as a formal sitting meditation for at least a few minutes at a time. That's how I suggest you do your first few mindfulness practice sessions.

Getting Started

Start by finding a quiet place, somewhere with the least possible distractions. Nowhere will be perfect, just find somewhere with relative quiet. You'll want to designate this as your dedicated meditation space. This can be a small spot in the corner of a room or even an entire room if you have one free and want to dedicate yourself to your practice (this kind of dedication doesn't have to, and won't likely, come right away). Remove all non-essential items from this spot so as to limit potential distractions.

Next, decide whether you'll set a timer or not and what you'll use to time your meditation session. This can be your smartphone, a simple clock if you rather not have your smartphone anywhere near you while meditating (smart idea), or a more formal meditation app which may allow you the functionality to log your sessions. For now, don't worry about the length of the meditation. In the beginning, you'll only be able to sit for a few minutes at a time and it's more important in the beginning to establish meditation as a daily habit than to try to sit for some lengthy period. You can start with just a few minutes at a time, even once a day. As to whether or not you should use a timer at all, you can go either way here. In the beginning, it's often more beneficial to not set a timer as the knowledge of this timer being on can cause you to grow restless in anticipation of your session finally being over. In the beginning, it's very difficult to sit because the mind is so active. This is so for everyone. *No, you're not averse to meditation. Yes, I'm talking to you.*

Next, I'd suggest getting a meditation cushion. It not only serves as a sign of your dedication to the practice, sending a signal to the mind that you take your practice seriously, but it serves the practical purpose of allowing you to adopt the most effective and comfortable sitting position while meditating. This cushion can be used to sit on the floor or in a chair. Choose whatever you believe will be a comfortable sitting position for you. If on the floor, sit on the front 1/3 of the pillow so that the back of the pillow bulges out behind you and allows you to straighten your back. If on a chair, you can do the same. If you'd like to keep it simple for now, you can simply sit on the floor in a cross-legged position or in a chair. Straighten your back and neck, place your hands in your lap, and look down three to four feet in front of you.

Now, either close your eyes or let your eyelids naturally fall so that they remain about half open. Keep in mind that eyes closed can make you more likely to fall asleep while meditating (a common problem), while eyes half-open may feel odd at first and distract you. For now, either is fine, but make it a point to find which works better for you.

Lastly, follow these four steps to practice mindful breathing:

1. Become aware of the breath

Simply turn your attention to your breath. Follow each in-breath and out-breath from beginning to end. Place a firm, but soft, focus on the breath. Do not attempt to control your breath, simply observe it silently. Your silent observation will slowly begin to calm your breathing naturally. This may be easier said than done in the beginning, but make your best effort.

2. Count each in-breath and out-breath

Inhale...one. Exhale.... two. Count to ten like this. If a thought distracts you, start the ten count over from one. When you get to ten, start over and attempt to count to ten again. If you never get there, don't worry. In the beginning, this will seem altogether impossible and it nearly is. The point isn't to get to ten in the beginning, but rather to quiet the mind. The time will come when you can do so, with practice.

Continue to do this for as many weeks or months as it takes until you can count to 10 with little to no effort. Then count each inhale + exhale as one. Then, when that becomes easy, stop counting and simply follow your breath. Don't rush this step, progress slowly. It can take months before you have the ability to even attempt this last step, and that's perfectly fine. Meditation isn't a competition and there's no way to lose or fail. Just do your best and you'll make your way.

3. Acknowledge thoughts, feelings, and sensations that arise

Understand in advance that various thoughts, feelings, and sensations will arise while being mindful and make you lose your concentration on the breath. This is perfectly normal and each should be welcomed in a spirit of open acceptance, as opposed to being critical and judgmental. This may be easier said than done in the beginning, but the important thing is that you're making the intention to do so.

In the beginning, you'll likely be interrupted constantly and feel as if you're doing something wrong. You're not and it really is that difficult for everyone, in the beginning, to stay concentrated on the breath.

4. Return to being mindful of the breath

As I've mentioned multiple times thus far, in the beginning, you'll lose focus on your breath constantly. Stay focused. After a while, your mind will begin to grow quieter. Return to the breath as many times as is necessary until your meditation session has ended (or until you feel as though you can't sit any longer, if you're not using a timer).

Keep in mind that while the practice won't necessarily feel easy in the beginning, it will get better, typically in a very short period of time. It's different for everyone, but, you'll often start noticing a calmer and quieter mind in just a few week's time.

Getting Off on the Right Foot

A few important tips for beginning with your mindful breathing practice:

1. In the beginning, it's about making meditation a daily habit.

Don't worry about how long your sessions are. Practice mindful breathing for just a few minutes (even one minute is fine) daily for the first one to two weeks. Really, in the beginning, nothing more is necessary and even with that you'll notice a difference. After a while, you'll feel gradually able to sit down for longer and longer periods. We'll talk more about making mindfulness a daily habit, later in Part I as well as about how to create an environment which helps make meditation a daily habit in *Easeful Discipline and Establishing a Daily Practice* of Part II.

2. Your mind will feel like a jungle. Don't sweat it.

I said this earlier, but, I feel it's important enough to mention again. People often feel like they're doing something wrong, like something's wrong with them, or like meditation just doesn't work for them. But, nothing is wrong at all. It's perfectly natural to feel like you're jumping out of your skin, unable to focus on one point for more than even 3 seconds. Everyone feels this way and you're not averse to meditation. This will quickly begin to change if you work to establish a consistent daily practice.

3. Be gentle with yourself throughout the process.

Don't go into the practice of mindfulness thinking that it's easy. It often isn't. In the beginning, you're likely to not notice clearly what is arising. You'll just know you've lost your concentration. At best, you'll know you were thinking about or feeling "something" but not know exactly what it was. But, there is the possibility that some uncomfortable thoughts and feelings can arise while meditating early on (this is more likely later). Be kind to yourself and know that whatever happens is totally natural and not a sign of any personal shortcoming.

Remember, the practice of mindful breathing is more than just a formal sitting meditation practice. Every day, every hour, and every moment you can go home to yourself in the present moment by becoming mindful of the breath. This is always available to you no matter how busy, hectic, or difficult your life becomes. Mindful breathing is a powerful tool for nourishing your well-being and serves as the foundation of your mindfulness practice.

Everyday Mindfulness

...you should make a great effort to bring the practice of mindfulness into your daily life.

I have three children. They're young (as of writing this, four years, two years, and just a few months old), crazy, and require a lot of time and effort to raise. As you might imagine, for now at least, I don't have a lot of time for "formal" sitting practice and find it pretty much impossible to slip away for extended meditation retreats. This is part of what attracted me to mindfulness practice. To know that I could bring the practice of meditation into my everyday life, as I walked, talked, ate, and even drove was truly a wonder to me.

Fundamentally, the practice of *This Moment* is to live fully present to our lives in each moment, both physically and mentally (which has layers to it- One Thing, One Mind, One Moment, and more). For this reason, you should make a great effort to bring the practice of mindfulness into your daily life. Without this, your practice is incomplete at best. Without being mindful in your everyday life, you'll miss the important points already outlined in the first three chapters and be incapable of living fully present to your life in this moment.

In this chapter, we'll cover the cornerstone mindfulness practices that will help you begin living a more mindful and fully present life. These practices, combined with mindful breathing both as a formal sitting meditation practice and as a practice which can be done at any time of day on the fly, make up the foundation of your mindfulness practice. This is because they make up the foundation of everything we do each day: breathing, walking, eating, communicating and moving in general. Then, in the next chapter, we'll take these practices and begin crafting a more defined and organized effort for bringing mindfulness into your daily life.

How to Practice: Mindful Walking

In order to have peace and joy, you must succeed in having peace within each of your steps. Your steps are the most important thing.

- Thich Nhat Hanh

Mindful walking is the second most common of all mindfulness practices and it's a personal favorite of mine. I feel mindful walking epitomizes mindfulness practice. Walking is one of the most common things we do each day, so the practice of walking mindfully is very powerful. To learn to walk mindfully in each moment is to ground ourselves in the peace and joy of the present moment time and time again, all throughout our day.

Mindful walking can be practiced both as a formal meditation practice (usually referred to as walking meditation) as well as an informal "everyday" practice. Walking meditation, the formal practice of mindful walking, can work as a highly effective "bridge" for bringing mindfulness into your daily life when practiced for a few minutes after each sitting meditation session. I'd suggest walking mindfully for at least a few minutes after each sitting meditation session. Even two to three minutes will help you begin to bring more mindfulness into your daily life.

A. Following Your Steps (Everyday Mindful Walking)

Mindful walking is one of the core mindfulness practices partly due to its ease of practice and great benefit. Like mindful breathing, opportunities to practice mindful walking are plentiful in daily life. This is the second of the Buddha's four postures, the first being sitting which we covered in the previous chapter and the third and fourth being standing and lying down (really, when you think about it, simply the four postures we can adopt at any moment in our life). This first practice is the "everyday" informal version of mindful walking, which is suited for any time you find yourself walking throughout your daily life.

1. Begin walking

A naturally slow pace is best. Walk slowly, but naturally. Keep in mind, you don't have to walk any particular speed when doing mindful walking. But, in the beginning, it will be necessary to slow down a bit. If you don't, you'll find it pretty much impossible to stay concentrated on your steps.

2. Follow your steps

This is really the essence of this form of walking meditation. Mindfully follow the movement of your left foot from the time you begin lifting the foot, as you transition to swinging it forward, and then as you place it back down. Then the same with the right foot back-and-forth. Mindful walking is really all about this sequence of being mindful of the lifting, swinging, and placing down of each foot, one after another. It's three movements, but you'll quickly realize that the act of following your steps is very fluid and that there is no separation between the movements. For this reason, it can be difficult to practice in the beginning. But, the more you practice, the more you'll clearly define each of the three individual movements. To help you stay mindful of your steps you can choose to count your steps just as you do in mindful breathing, one count for each step.

3. Acknowledge that which arises + return

Throughout your walk you'll be concentrated on your steps. But, because this is mindfulness practice, your awareness should be open and welcoming. Just as we talked about with mindful breathing, openly accept all thoughts, feelings, and sensations as they arise. Then, having momentarily acknowledged what has arisen, simply return to your steps.

B. Walking Meditation (Formal Practice)

Formal walking meditation practice is all about counting your steps, at least at first. This makes it the easiest mindful walking practice of all. Like counting your breath, counting your steps is all about counting each step as 1 (left 1, right 2, left 3) until you get to 10.

1. Begin walking at a naturally slow pace.

It's important to walk at a specified pace in walking meditation. Whatever that is, stick to that pace throughout. Most choose to do this practice very slowly, although that's not required. If you're just starting out, stick to a slow pace.

2. Posture & positioning

Walk with good posture and bring your hands up to around your diaphragm. Place your left hand up against your diaphragm and your right hand directly in front of it, then allow your thumbs to cross so that your left thumb is in front and your right thumb is against your body. Your forearms should be horizontal with the ground. This hand positioning helps balance and stabilize you while walking.

3. Match your steps to your breath

Breathe naturally and pay attention to how many naturally slow steps you take for each in-breath and each out-breath. The in-breath tends to be shorter, so keep that in mind (in-breath may be 3 steps, while out-breath is 4).

4. Count your steps

Now that you know how many steps you're taking for each in-breath and out-breath, count them. There are various ways this can be done:

1. *Counting numbers:* 1-2-3, 1-2-3-4, 1-2-3, 1-2-3-4.
2. *Sides:* Left-right-left, right-left-right-left, right-left-right, left-right-left-right.
3. *In-breath-out-breath:* In-breath, out-breath, in-breath, out-breath.

5. Be mindful

Be fully present as you count each left step and each right step. You're being mindful of the count here most of all, that's what you're concentrating on. You can be mindful of the movement of your legs in between counts as well if you're walking at a slow pace.

6. Acknowledge that which arises + return

Just the same as with following your steps, acknowledge any thoughts, feelings, and sensations which arise and then go back to your steps.

How to Practice: Mindful Eating

Mindful eating is another core mindfulness practice. The reason why is easy to see. Every day, multiple times per day, we eat. This alone makes it an ideal mindfulness practice. But, there's more to it than just that.

When we eat, we're generally partaking in something we enjoy doing. Typically, we eat something we enjoy the flavor of, and that flavor, as well as the texture and visual appeal, are all things which we can notice with our mindfulness. Also, the act of chewing lends itself to mindfulness because it's a repetitive process done by the physical body just like walking and breathing (these repetitive, or at least constantly moving, processes are important for an ideal mindfulness practice).

Mindful eating is a very beneficial practice because it allows us to pay very close attention to what we put into our body and how we do it. Many people develop bad habits in connection with food, and it's mindful eating which allows us to notice those harmful patterns of behavior so that we can make a change. Also, mindful eating allows us to become more closely connected with the food we place into our body, which comes from all around the world and is a great example of the interbeing nature of all things which you can tap into when eating a meal. This is a very nourishing exercise.

But, more than anything, mindful eating allows us to live more fully in the present moment. We eat multiple times each and every day, so eating mindfully is not only a nourishing practice in itself but also encourages mindful living outside of eating as well.

1. Pause

Take a moment before eating to notice the aroma, visual appeal, and texture of the food. Savor the various sensations which accompany your meal. This short moment will help your awareness open up so that you become more fully present to the act of eating.

2. Eat mindfully

Be mindful of the lifting of your hand or utensil and the act of chewing the food itself. Pay close attention to each flavor in your mouth and notice how the food feels and smells as you chew it. As your primary point of concentration during mindful eating, be fully present for the act of chewing. Attempt to chew each bite 20-30 times (depending on the food you're eating this may not be possible).

3. Acknowledge thoughts, feelings, and sensations + return

When thoughts, feelings, or other sensations arise within your field of awareness, simply be mindful of them, openly and welcomingly acknowledge their presence, and then allow them to pass as if they were floating by on a cloud. Then, bring your focus back to the act of chewing. You'll lose your concentration constantly in the beginning. Don't worry, this is normal for any form of mindfulness practice. Simply repeat steps two through three and attempt to eat mindfully for as much of your meal as possible.

How to Practice: Mindful Communication

Another major mindfulness practice, and one which isn't talked about enough, is mindful communication. This is for two reasons:

1. Mindful communication expands the meaning of mindfulness practice to a small degree (in a positive way), so it's not an obvious practice.
2. Mindful communication can be difficult.

It can be very difficult to know what to concentrate on when speaking or listening to another in conversation. How can we practice mindfulness when communicating? There's so much going on in that moment, both in our head, our body, and outside in the world.

Mindful communication is not a traditional mindfulness practice, because it's more applying aspects of mindfulness practice to communication than anything. But, to ignore communication in our overall practice of mindful living is a great mistake, not only because of how prolific communication is in our life but also because we can easily apply many of the principles of mindfulness practice to communication if we just look a little more closely. Ultimately, mindful communication is different from other mindfulness practices such as mindful breathing and walking, but only in a subtle way. For the most part, it's the same practice we do when breathing and walking. To practice mindful communication is to practice the art of paying attention to this moment. Specifically, in speech that means paying attention to:

- The thoughts and feelings that go through your mind, before and after you speak. Is there anger, fear, or jealousy or compassion and loving-kindness?
- Sensations in your body, such as tenseness or nervousness.
- The intention of the words you speak. Were you trying to cause harm? Make up for a perceived lack of confidence in yourself? Make someone else feel inadequate so that you could get ahead? Or were you trying to make them feel better or encourage them?
- And the result of those words: Did they cause harm? Did they clue you in on something else within you? Did they encourage or help calm the other person?

The easiest way to remember how to practice mindful speech is to remember that it originates with you. At first, pay attention to your physical body, your thoughts, and the intentions behind them and your practice of mindful speech will develop. Once you've spoken, though, pay attention to the effect that your words had on the other person. Were they hurt, confused, encouraged, or calmed by your words? Because mindfulness practice is incomplete without the practice of compassion and loving-kindness, which we'll talk about in Part IV in more detail, it's important to pay attention to whether your words have harmed or helped the other person and work to change that if they're the former.

With regards to mindful listening, the opportunity to be mindful is more clear. When listening, there is a constant stream of something being directed towards us with which we can "latch" onto (concentrate on) and be mindful of: the other person's voice. Concentrate on the person's voice and on the words they're speaking. Really make an effort to listen with your entire being to the words spoken, as opposed to what most of us usually do, which is to think in our heads as the other person speaks and wait for our next chance to speak (especially when arguing). So, in mindful listening, you pay attention more to the other person than anything else, but it once again goes back to you. This is because what you're really looking for is the effect the words are having on you:

- Is what the other person is saying hurting you, making you angry, fearful, joyful, peaceful, or confused?
- What thoughts, other feelings, or sensations arise in connection with their words?

Mindful communication is a great opportunity to tune into hidden bias, prejudice, and other wrong perceptions. And because we communicate each and every day constantly, mindful communication is another very powerful practice, albeit one which is slightly different from other mindfulness practices which involve concentration on one static point for extended periods. But, as I mentioned a moment ago, with the significance of communication in our daily lives, to ignore communication would be a mistake. To adopt mindful communication is to further deepen your mindful living practice and improve the quality of your life by improving the quality of your communication.

How to Practice: 7 Mindful Movements

Anything can be done with mindfulness. You can cook, clean, eat, drink, walk, drive, speak, listen, exercise, and do anything else mindfully. Once you get the hang of mindfulness practice, you can see this clearly and know how to practice anything in mindfulness, even if you haven't been given instruction.

For that reason, beyond mindful breathing, walking, eating, and communicating, it can be very beneficial to begin conditioning your body to become accustomed to moving mindfully throughout your daily life in a general way. This is one of the major purposes of the 7 Mindful Movements exercise, which conditions your body to grow accustomed to moving more mindfully as opposed to always operating on auto-pilot.

I designed this specific routine, which is essentially a routine of 7 different stretches resembling Yoga, after studying the movement routines of Zen master Thich Nhat Hanh's Plum Village monastery and the similar application of Yoga by Jon Kabat-Zinn in the Mindfulness-Based Stress Reduction program, combined with increasing awareness of the very real health dangers of sitting.

In an age where almost everyone sits either at work or home for long hours each day (and for some of us, almost all day), the dangers of sitting are profound and very real, as James A. Levine, M.D., Ph.D. of Mayoclinc.org reported[2]:

Research has linked sitting for long periods of time with a number of health concerns, including obesity and metabolic syndrome — a cluster of conditions that includes increased blood pressure, high blood sugar, excess body fat around the waist and abnormal cholesterol levels. Too much sitting also seems to increase the risk of death from cardiovascular disease and cancer.

One study compared adults who spent less than two hours a day in front of the TV or other screen-based entertainment with those who logged more than four hours a day of recreational screen time. Those with greater screen time had:

- A nearly 50 percent increased risk of death from any cause
- About a 125 percent increased risk of events associated with cardiovascular disease, such as chest pain (angina) or heart attack

The increased risk was separate from other traditional risk factors for cardiovascular disease, such as smoking or high blood pressure.

And the effects of moving more often are just as profound:

The impact of movement — even leisurely movement — can be profound. For starters, you'll burn more calories. This might lead to weight loss and increased energy. Even better, the muscle activity needed for standing and other movement seems to trigger important processes related to the breakdown of fats and sugars within the body. When you sit, these processes stall — and your health risks increase. When you're standing or actively moving, you kick the processes back into action.

For those not particularly concerned with their physical health, this may not seem like a huge deal. But, consider the fact that getting up and moving more has the ability to increase our energy and vitality levels each day and you've now drawn a direct connection between moving more often and living more fully in each moment.

But, this is just the beginning. The 7 Mindful Movement routine is most importantly about helping us make it a habit to move more mindfully each day. By doing this

This Moment

routine I've noticed that I'm not just more mindful throughout each day, I'm now more deeply in touch with my body than I've ever been before. Moving mindfully is a nice change of pace and a very enjoyable practice which helps us live more mindfully and connect with our bodies in a very intimate way. And this connecting with our bodies through mindful movement has the ability to help us better manage physical pain, as Louise Hunt of Charted Society of Physiotherapy (*csp.org.uk*) reported[3]:

In chronic pain intervention, mindfulness involves using meditation to create moment-by-moment awareness of the body and thoughts. The aim is to make a distinction between primary and secondary suffering. Similar principles can be applied in managing depression, anxiety or long-term conditions.

The distinction between primary and secondary suffering is fundamental to mindfulness. Primary suffering is, for example, the unpleasant sensations of back pain, whereas secondary suffering is all the negative reactions associated with pain that can lead to fear, depression and further tension producing additional pain.

Vidyamala Burch is the founder of the not-for-profit firm Breathworks, which provides courses in mindfulness. She says: 'With mindfulness you can learn to accept the primary pain and reduce the secondary suffering, which can sometimes radically reduce pain. A lot of secondary pain is about resistance, we say to ourselves "I don't want this" and everything gets worse. Mindfulness can pull you out of the pit of chronic suffering.'

Suffice it to say, moving mindfully is a highly beneficial practice. And you can adopt a very simple version of this practice each day that takes all but 10 minutes to complete. Do each movement (somewhat) slowly and mindfully, paying very close attention to the specific movement of the body. With exception of the bow, which is done once in the beginning and once at the end, do each of the other six movements three times each before moving on to the next movement:

1. Start: The bow

The bow is the beginning and end of the 7 Mindful Movements routine. This involves standing up straight with your feet together and either bowing with your hands held together at chest height in a praying/namaste/gassho position (it's all the same) or with your hands at their side. Bow slowly, mindfully, being fully present as you lower your upper body just above waist height. Then, come back up. Every little movement of the entire routine should be done mindfully with your entire being.

This bow is a great movement to start with because it's simple and prepares the body for movement, also putting you into the right state of mind, but also because it holds a lot of significance. To bow is to shed the ego. It is to give up the little "I" in exchange for the big "I" and expand ourselves beyond the small scope we often hold ourselves to. It's unfortunate Western culture has such an allergy to bowing due to our ego-centricity, because it's a truly nourishing practice in itself without anything tied to it.

2. Heart

Heart is a side-to-side movement in which you'll be making the shape of a heart by lifting your arms up sideways from resting at your sides until they're horizontal, essentially with you then holding your arms out as if to show your wingspan. Your palms should be facing up towards the sky.

From there, lift your lower-arms from the elbow down up until they're vertical and let your hands curl in towards the body and move downward until you touch your shoulders with the tips of your fingers. In this way, you make a sort of heart shape with the movement of your arms from start to finish.

Lastly, allow your lower arms to go back to their horizontal position with your upper arms and then bring your entire arms completely back down to your side. Complete this movement three times.

3. Circle

Circle is a front-to-back movement. Remember that exercise they had you do in school where you swung your arms around in circles at their side like your arms were propellers? It's essentially that movement with a twist.

Starting once again with your arms at their side, begin swinging your arms back, then upward, then start moving back down towards the front of your body almost as if to make circles with the swinging of your arms, but as you come back down and your arms move from being behind your body to over your head and then in front of your body, allow your hands to come together once again as we did in the bow (if you did the prayer position), rest for a moment at chest height, and then separate once again and go back down to your side.

Complete this movement three times.

4. Balance

This movement is a simple leg swing. Bring your hands up and let them rest at your waist as if you were resting from having just ran long distance. If you find it hard to balance like this (once you start lifting your leg), you can extend your arms out horizontally as we did in movement one, Heart.

Now, with legs still together, raise your left leg up sideways away from the body a few feet (about as far as it will go while allowing you to maintain good balance). Then, bring the leg back down. Do this leg three times before moving on to the next. Then, do the same for the right leg three times.

5. Grounding

Grounding is a simple squat exercise. Separate your feet until they're about shoulder-width apart and raise your arms out in front of you with palms facing down.

Next, begin lowering your body down to the ground with your legs in a squat motion. As you drop yourself to the floor imagine yourself becoming grounded with the Earth and very strong. Stop once your upper legs (thighs) are parallel with the ground. Or, if you can't go that far, until you feel you're as low as you can go. Complete this movement three times.

6. Stepping Back

Stepping Back is a slider reverse lunge exercise, and it's simply the act of sliding one leg back as far as it will go. Bring your hands up to your waist just as you did in movement #3, Balance. Then, begin sliding your left foot backward from the balls of your feet some three to four feet back until your right leg starts to go down as well (almost to where you're on one knee). Don't go too far if it's uncomfortable, the point isn't to push your body too hard but simply to be fully present for the movement itself, so just slide your foot back until you feel the stretch, hold it for a moment, and then bring it back. Complete this movement three times before moving on to the right leg.

7. Rising Up

Rising Up is a thoracic bridge exercise and definitely the most difficult move in the routine. If you find yourself unable to perform this movement, feel free to skip it.

First, begin by getting down on all fours with your head facing down to the ground. Make sure to continue to be mindful throughout the entire routine, even as you change positions. Next, let your left leg move to the opposite side of your right leg at the same time that you pick your right arm up from the ground and point it parallel to the ground to the right of you. At the same time as you move your arm, allow your chest to go from pointing down to the ground to turning up to where it's pointing out sideways, the same direction as your horizontal right arm. When you do this movement, your entire body will essentially spin around upward along with your pelvic bone and legs. Make sure to raise your pelvic bone up towards the sky so that your body isn't slouching. Now, your head, chest, and right arm will be pointing out sideways to the right, your feet will be pointing the opposite from their original direction, and your pelvic area, abdomen, and upper legs pointing upwards towards the sky. Your left arm should stay in the same place the entire time.

Next, simply do the reverse and bring your body back to the original all-fours position it was in and do the opposite side. Complete this movement three times on each side. It might sound difficult, but once you get the hang of the exercise it's very simple to do and very powerful. It's not only great for your health, but because of the complexity of the movement it's a great addition to the mindful movement routine and the perfect movement to finish with.

End: Bow

Simply do movement #1, the bow, once again to complete the routine. Once completed, make sure to take a

This Moment

moment to pay attention to your body and become present to the fact that you've just completed the routine.

Making Mindfulness a Way of Life

To make mindfulness a way of life, an all-around effort is necessary from practice, to strategy, to the right mental attitude.

There's more to making mindfulness a way of life, to changing that habitual set point, than just the practice of mindfulness itself. Anything can be done with mindful awareness. Technically, you could be mindful 24 hours a day. But, to actually do this is much, much easier said than done. Even to do a fraction of that requires great effort. To make mindfulness a way of life, an all-around effort is necessary from practice, to strategy, to the right mental attitude. That's what this chapter is about. Specifically, strategies for helping support the major effort of practicing mindfulness throughout your daily life.

Making mindfulness a way of life is about moving your habitual set point from "mindless" to more often "mindful". This is one of the most important efforts in mindfulness practice. It's best to imagine it as a sort of sliding scale:

Mindless _____X_____Mindful

This Moment

At any given moment in your life, your set point is the average of each mindless & mindful moment over a particular point in time. This is a bit of an over simplification of mindfulness practice, but it gets a very important point across: you're continually working to undo the habit of mindlessness, or adopt the habit of mindfulness, in your daily life.

Unfortunately, very quickly I discovered that it's not so easy to live mindfully. To truly live in a way that we walk, talk, eat, and drive mindfully, even some of the time, is a great effort. As beneficial as it is, to make mindfulness a way of life is against our habitual patterns. Our habitual patterns of living mindlessly, rushing around, and cutting corners to be productive and get the job done are all hurdles to cross. All of these things get in the way of you living a more mindful life and there's no other way to handle them other than to work on them slowly but surely, each day, and one step at a time. But, working to make mindfulness a way of life is a worthy effort, one of the most important efforts of anyone's life in my opinion and a foundational effort of the practice outlined in *This Moment*. As we've talked about already, it leads to so many important developments in the mind and in our overall well-being that it's difficult to imagine living the rest of one's life without it. And the great thing is, if you can cultivate the ability to live even 5% of your life more mindfully, you'll notice a significant change in the quality of your day-to-day experience.

In this chapter, we'll be covering how to cultivate a more mindful lifestyle via a set of seven step instructions, three valuable practices for living more mindfully amid the distractions and busyness of daily life, and a simple exercise I call Reaffirming Your Practice for when you fall off your practice of mindful living and need to get back on the horse so to speak, something we all face from time to time.

Creating a More Mindful Lifestyle

The following are seven steps, all of which I've used personally, each helping in their own unique way towards living a more mindful lifestyle:

1. Meditate twice a day

This may seem like a simple point, but it's one of the most important. Your formal sitting meditation practice emphasizes your daily mindfulness practice, so if instead of meditating once a day you meditate twice a day and space those sessions out as morning & afternoon or morning & night, you'll notice your ability to be mindful throughout the rest of your day improve. This second session doesn't have to be as long as you're first, too. If you're first session is 30 minutes, you can simply choose to do a second 10-15-minute session. It's completely up to you, just so long as you get yourself on the cushion that second time each day.

2. Start simple with a focus practice

This is about focusing in on one major "everyday" informal activity for an entire week, such as walking or eating, making it a point to focus on doing only that activity mindfully and not worrying about any other informal practice (although welcoming it when you do remember). By focusing in this way, you simplify the practice and make it easier to stick to. When we first begin practicing, living mindfully can seem like a daunting task and has the ability to discourage us. But, by choosing a focus practice, you can relieve much of that burden and take the practice one major daily activity at a time. Good examples of major daily activities to pick are walking, eating, or driving (if you do a lot of driving, or at least drive daily).

After one to two weeks you can choose to add a second activity, but only if you feel you've begun to get the first down.

If not, simply continue for another week until you feel comfortable. This really helps simplify the process of bringing mindfulness into your everyday life by simplifying the practice and removing the expectation to be mindful during other activities, which often helps us more than anything else.

3. Schedule little moments of mindfulness

The most important point to mention here is the practice of going home to yourself throughout each day. Remember that we talked about mindful breathing as a practice which can be done anywhere and at any time. If you simply set a reminder to go off on your smartphone every hour or two (while you're awake, of course) and go home to your breath, breathing mindfully for a minute or two, you'll notice a significant improvement in your ability to be mindful throughout your daily life. This may sound like a very simple practice, and it is, but it's absolutely one of the most powerful and the practice you're likely to use more than any other (that is, simply stopping to breathe mindfully for short moments throughout your day).

4. Set up reminders

Reminders are a simple, but very powerful, tool for making mindfulness a way of life. Mindfulness is the very practice of remembering, to remember to be present and concentrate on whatever your point of concentration is. For this reason, reminders serve as the most natural aid in bringing mindfulness to your daily life.

In the beginning of your mindfulness practice, you'll likely find it very difficult to remember to be mindful throughout the day, so simple reminders work like a charm. These can come in many forms, probably the easiest and most accessible being phone reminders. I'd suggest using a unique sound for the reminder, something you don't use for anything else, that way you begin to associate the sound specifically with remembering to be mindful throughout your day. This is essentially what we just spoke about in point #3, so refer to that for the first point on this list.

There are various types of reminders that can be utilized:

1. *Timed reminders*: See point #3.

2. *Physical reminders:* This can be something such as a poster on your bedroom or office wall with a quote that compels you to be mindful, a wallpaper on your smartphone, or a piece of jewelry, such as a bracelet or necklace, that symbolizes your practice.

3. *Momentum Browser Extension*: If you use the internet often (as most of us do), especially if you use it for work, then that can be a great source for distraction from your practice. To keep this from happening, use the Momentum browser extension (only works on the Chrome browser). This simple extension changes the "new tab" page to a simple page with the time, date, a blank line to type in a message (such as "be mindful"), and a beautiful wallpaper in the background. It really helps keep you from being distracted while online and serves as a powerful reminder to be mindful.

4. *Mindfulness Bell Browser Extension (Chrome + Firefox)*: This is another browser extension which is very powerful, but this one works on Chrome and Firefox. This is the perfect aid to practice if you utilize point #3, scheduling little moments of mindfulness, because it allows you to set a timer to go off every so often in which a traditional Buddhist-themed bell will sound with a little message to remind you to go home to your breath

that will pop up in the top right corner of the screen. I use this every day and highly recommend it.

5. Prioritize mindfulness

This is a big topic in Part II, *Living Intentionally*, so I won't go into detail here, but know that this is one of the most important points. To bring the practice of mindfulness into your life but not treat it with a certain level of importance is a surefire way to fall off your practice and never get back on.

To stick with your practice and make mindfulness a way of life, you need to treat it with a certain level of importance. What are your priorities? What's most important to you? Quite often what we prioritize (because we all have priorities, whether you decided them intentionally or not) isn't in line with what's most important to us. Cleaning that broken picture up is a very important part of making mindfulness a way of life. You need to decide that your mindfulness practice is a priority and then act that way in your daily life.

6. Let go of expectations (Go easy on yourself and be patient)

This is another very important point. The reality is, we all come to mindfulness practice wanting something out of it. This is perfectly natural. No one has ever come to any spiritual practice of any kind without an expectation to "get" something for themselves. But, it doesn't mean it's not harmful.

Because of these expectations, we decide in our mind that we should get something at a certain point in time. The problem occurs when that doesn't happen. When the expectation isn't met. It's then that we beat ourselves up and lose the motivation to practice. Don't beat yourself up over having expectations. As I mentioned, it's natural to have them. All you can do is let go of them when you notice them arise. Notice the expectation arise, acknowledge it, and decide in your mind that you're going to let go of it and let your practice develop on its own. Simply allow this to be another part of your mindfulness practice.

7. Find, or grow, a mindful community

In Buddhism, the sangha is one of the most important principles of all. Buddhists understand the importance of a community working together towards a unified goal and utilize it masterfully. But, whether you're Buddhist or not, this is an important principle to utilize. Finding a community of practitioners isn't necessarily easy, and it doesn't have to be your focus in the beginning, but it is something very important to stay aware of, eventually with the intention to fulfill it in one way or another.

Depending on what you're interested in, you may search out a center for a specific school of Buddhism, a monastery, a secular meditation center, or simply a local meditation meet-up with a small group of people (typically at someone's home or a rented space at a community center). Here are some options to get you started:

- *Shambhala Buddhist centers:* http://shambhala.org/centres/find-shambhala-centre/
- *Plum Village sangha directory, Zen master Thich Nhat Hanh's tradition*: http://www.mindfulnessbell.org/directory.php
- *Wake Up! meet up groups, also Zen master Thich Nhat Hanh's tradition*: http://www.wkup.org/get-involved/
- *Also*: a simple Google search with your state/nearest major city plus "meditation center", "mindfulness center", "Buddhist center", or "Buddhist monastery" (depending on what you're looking for) is a good start.

Living Mindfully with Distraction and Busyness

Practicing mindfulness and developing a daily meditation practice in the fast-paced and plugged-in modern world can be pretty difficult. I struggled with this for a long time, trying to figure out ways to be mindful throughout more of my day and stop the habitual rushing around I had done for years. There's the complexity of modern life, the habitual patterns we're trying to get ourselves out of, and the constant distractions that try to pull us away. Even if you see amazing results from your mindfulness practice, it can still be difficult to resist these forces. I went through this myself repeatedly and often got so frustrated I just felt like stopping. I knew it didn't make sense. I'd discovered a sense of peace and happiness from my practice that I hadn't felt by doing anything else in my life, but I just couldn't get myself to practice consistently. I knew there had to be a way to make it work. It took a while to figure it out, and while it can be difficult no matter what you do (life, and any old habitual patterns, love to get in the way), I've figured out many different little steps that can help you get there with less headache than I had to go through.

When it comes to making meditation, and being mindful in your daily life, a habit, there are various factors you have to consider. Don't ever think you've tried everything, because there's so much you can do to improve your practice and bring more mindfulness into your daily life, even if you run a typical nine-to-five and have loads of responsibility. We've talked about an entire plan for bringing mindfulness into your daily life so far, but here are three more highly effective steps you can take that specifically help when dealing with the heavy distractions and busyness of modern life:

1. Make driving a time for meditation

If there's one place we'd almost never think of being present, it's driving. I don't mean you don't pay attention (even then a lot of us drive half-asleep...), I mean more-so driving without being present of your own mind and body. Driving meditation is a really great practice that can help transform something we usually only do to get from place to place (or one event in our life to the next) into something you look forward to and find peace and joy in doing. It's the perfect time to put a "stop" to your day (while you're going) and become present.

How to Practice: Mindful Driving

1. Allow your awareness to remain relatively "open"

While you're driving, there will be multiple objects that will "pull" your attention away. Know that this is just how it is, and allow your awareness to "open up" and accept these various things into your field of awareness (the street signs, traffic) whenever necessary, acknowledging them and then shifting back to your object of concentration.

2. Concentrate on your hands or feet

While driving, you can shift between being mindful of your hands on the steering wheel, making little "micro" turns to keep the car centered, as well as of your foot on the pedal, moving up and down constantly. Each are relatively constant movements, which make them decent targets to use as anchors while being mindful (just as you use your breathing while practicing mindful breathing, or your steps during mindful walking).

3. Acknowledge openly

As always, you're being mindful, so acknowledge anything that arises within your mind or body while being mindful in an open and accepting way. Just be and watch silently for what arises. It's so easy and convenient to practice mindful driving, and when you're driving, what better to do?

2. Give yourself more time to get from place to place

Most of us are accustomed to rushing around and that environment makes it more difficult to practice mindfulness throughout your daily life. From now on, leave five to ten minutes earlier than normal so that you can take your time to drive, walk, and do anything you have to do more mindfully. To take it a step further, give yourself more time to get ready as well if there's any prep needed before you leave.

Now, you might be saying, "Well. that doesn't work. That will take more of my time." If that's your answer, you probably need to reanalyze your priorities (which we'll talk about in Part II: *Living Intentionally*). Of course, this won't always be possible, but most of the time it's easy to do so. I do a lot each day and, provided I plan accordingly, I'm almost never in a position where I have to rush around to get everything done. It's just a mindset, something we convince ourselves is necessary, but really isn't. Give yourself more time to prep and travel and find more time to breathe and be mindful.

3. Arrive, wherever you go

Arriving is a technique which involves you becoming present as you're about to enter a new area and allowing your mind to fully "arrive" in that location once you've entered.

The reason arriving can help you live more mindfully is because it's not a lengthy or continuous practice you have to do, it's simply the quick and habitual act of becoming fully present as you leave one area and enter another. And by doing so, each time you enter a new place (whether that's inside work, home, the store, or when walking outside from somewhere else), you'll not only remind yourself constantly throughout the day to be mindful (and if you've practiced for some time you know simply remembering to be mindful throughout your busy day is one of the greatest challenges), but by reminding yourself throughout each day you'll naturally end up actually being mindful more often. It's always two-fold with mindfulness and reminders. When you arrive somewhere fully with body and mind you become present, and you'll then often continue to be mindful for at least a few moments after that.

Then, on top of that, simply reminding yourself more often throughout each day means you stay aware of your practice more often and remember to practice at other random times outside of when you're "arriving".

How to Practice: Mindful Arriving

1. Leave

As you walk up to a door or entry way, become present to the fact that you're leaving this area that you're currently walking in. This isn't always easy, because we may have just fought with our spouse or another loved one or had a hard time at work. But, no matter what happened, remember that the past has come and gone and you now have a fresh new moment with which to move on to and live fully in.

2. Enter

Now, be mindful as you place your hands on the door knob/handle and open the door/walk through the door way. Open this door with both hands, fully with your entire being. Know that you're entering this new area. This also isn't always easy. Sometimes, we dread walking through a door and know that what may be waiting for us on the other side is only more pain and suffering. So, as you enter this near area, consciously allow yourself to open up to the moment fully and reaffirm that you're present to this moment no matter what it holds. No expectations, no assumptions, just an open acceptance of whatever may come.

3. Arrive

Once you've stepped in, be mindful of the fact that you've just left the previous area and are now fully in this new area. Know that you've arrived and are present for whatever may come.

Arriving is a great practice because it makes sure that each new place you step into you arrive in a mindful state, and that's a great foundation for any mindfulness practice and your life as a whole.

Reaffirming Your Practice

To make mindfulness a way of life, you need to be willing to fail. Or, at least, to accept when you don't go through with what you have planned for yourself. This is because, no matter how hard you try, no matter how much effort you put in, you'll fall of your practice constantly. Very quickly, you need to understand that this is a natural part of the practice and not something which points to your own lack of capability. If you can do this, you'll make your way just fine, gradually, to a more mindful life.

In the beginning of my practice, I'd sometimes go days without even the slightest thought of being, or reminder to be, mindful. I'd get frustrated and beat myself up, feeling defeated that I couldn't do what seemed like such a simple effort. But, simple doesn't mean easy. As time went on, I began to live more mindfully, slowly but surely, but I realized something. Those moments of falling off never stop happening. At least, in most cases. It was for this reason that I adopted what I'd later call Reaffirming Your Practice.

Reaffirming your practice is the simple practice of reestablishing yourself after you've fallen off your practice. For a day, a week, or longer. This can be simply due to the difficulty of the practice or due to other circumstances. However long it's been, and for whatever reason, you can reaffirm your practice, strengthen your resolve, root yourself in your practice once again, and continue on.

How to Practice: Reaffirming Your Practice

Reaffirming your practice is the practice of starting anew when you've fallen off your practice of mindful living. The reality is, you're going to fall off from time-to-time. When that happens, you have only two choices:

1. Quit and move on, leaving behind your practice and giving up taking care of yourself. A recipe sure for future pain and suffering.

2. Keep going by remembering the significance of what it is that you're doing, of the teaching or the knowledge itself, of the teachers that have taught you or brought you along the path, or of the community which supports or has supported you if you have one.

The one defining characteristic of a Buddhist across all schools of Buddhism is the ritual of having taken refuge in the "three jewels" of the Buddha (the teacher), the Dharma (the teaching), and the Sangha (the community), which essentially means to symbolically root oneself in these three principles as one's guides along the path.

If you're Buddhist, it's the three jewels which you initially take refuge in and it's the three jewels which you find refuge in each time you encounter a difficult point on your journey. If you're not Buddhist, don't worry, because the practice of taking refuge and reaffirming your practice is something anyone can take advantage of. Remember who introduced this practice to you, who has taught you along the way, someone specific to this challenge you're facing along your path. Remember the practice itself. Remember the importance of mindfulness and of living intentionally, naturally, and with compassion and loving-kindness and the significance behind these teachings (and any other teachings of importance to you). And remember anyone who supports you along this path. Take time to be with them, to open up to them and allow yourself to take refuge in their support.

There are many ways to reaffirm your practice. However you decide to do so, it's important to have this as a tool which you can utilize when you encounter challenges along the path (as well as to be that for others when they need it). Reaffirm your practice constantly, however often you need. This is a completely renewable practice. Falling and then getting back up again is the nature of life, not just mindfulness and meditation practice, so lean in to the practice and know

This Moment

that if you fall you can always get back up. You always have the ability to rise again, no matter how tough it becomes.

Making Friends with Yourself

The journey to yourself is the path you walk in mindfulness practice.

What does it mean to make friends with yourself? What does it mean to make friends with anyone? I mean *best friends*. Fundamentally, it's the process of opening up the pathways of communication and getting to know that person intimately. Making friends with yourself is, firstly, the act of opening up to yourself. This is done right from the get-go with mindfulness practice to some degree, but there needs to be further emphasis on openly accepting whatever we may be confronted with because of that practice. Next, it's about the process of getting to know ourselves in the deepest and most intimate way. This is what I often call the *journey to yourself.*

The journey to yourself is the path you walk in mindfulness practice. It's the path we walk in life in a lot of ways, but with mindfulness it's far more defined and we're less likely to hold ourselves back due to internal blocks such as fear. This journey to yourself is a life-long journey, one which has both bright spots and dark ones. It's through this journey that we come face-to-face with our "demons".

This Moment

The reality is, most of us are our own worst enemy. We harbor an internal dialogue that beats us down at every turn, telling us twenty different shades of, "you're not good enough", over and over again, each and every day. Also, we never take the time to nourish our mind or even attempt to heal the wounds we feel within ourselves. The most we ever do is distract ourselves with various physical and mental intoxicants to bottle down the pain or run from it. However, this leads to a lot of pain and suffering and these issues will never just work themselves out. We need to take the time to turn inward and work on ourselves, otherwise nothing will ever happen. It starts with us. We need to become our own best friend. And we do that by diligently following the journey to ourselves.

Imagine, for a moment, that you're traveling through a forest. And while you're travelling through this forest, you have a light. This light, this torch, which you hold along your journey, is the light of mindfulness. As you walk throughout this forest- the forest of the mind- the light of mindfulness helps light your way. When you walk through an open clearing and can view the sun, this light makes your trip all the more enjoyable, allowing you to appreciate and take joy in the warmth and light of the sun. When you're walking through a dark path, this torch lights your way and keeps you from walking off the path into a dangerous place. No matter where you are, this light guides you. Imagine for a moment, walking through this dark forest with nothing. No light whatsoever. You'd have no idea where you were. You wouldn't know West from East nor would you be able to properly navigate yourself out of this dark place. This is what it's like when we attempt to navigate our lives without mindfulness.

The path never becomes easy and we never stop having to walk through dark patches of forest, but with the light of mindfulness we gain an ally along the path that allows us to better navigate these challenges and properly take care of ourselves.

Entering the Forest

When you first begin your mindfulness practice, you're entering the forest. Think of a time when you went somewhere amazing for the first time. Everything was new and the entire experience was almost overwhelming. So much is unknown, so much is just being learned, but it's all being taken in fully because it's fresh and new. This is, in many ways, what it's like to begin on the journey to yourself with mindfulness practice.

In the beginning, you'll notice various thoughts, feelings, and sensations arise within you during practice, but you'll rarely, if ever, be able to identify clearly what is arising. It will likely feel new and interesting and altogether different from anything else you've ever experienced.

But after some time, you'll begin to notice specific thoughts and feelings. You may notice fear from time to time, or anger, or anxiety. Whatever it is, you've begun to gain some relative level of clarity. It doesn't always feel comfortable, but you've experienced enough of the beauty of your practice already to know this is the right path. You've now begun progressing down the path, but this is just the beginning.

The Dark Path

With greater and greater clarity comes the ability to notice what's arising. That is, to notice specifically what's arising. It's not a feeling, it's fear. It's not fear, it's your fear of failure. And it's not just your fear of failure- it's your fear of failure, fear of failure, fear of failure, fear of failure...it's your internal dialogue, repeating this message of "you're a failure" over and over again. This is where you've arrived now and it will take every ounce of your skillfulness to navigate the path.

However, this isn't just some dark and difficult path which you're bound to walk forever, this is a new challenge which you need to learn how to properly navigate. Doing so makes life *easier*, not more difficult. Although initially it may feel more difficult.

By bringing together the right ingredients, we can find a way to more skillfully navigate this path and transform it from that of darkness to one of both light and dark, constantly at play with one another in harmony. This is the ability to navigate life itself with greater peace and joy in each moment. This ability to properly navigate not just the good moments, but the difficult, is a big part of what allows us to live fully and freely in this moment.

Becoming Your Own Best Friend

At this point, it's important to mention a few key ingredients that need to be in place for this path you walk to be as easeful and effective as possible. It's not enough just to be mindful, you also need to walk the path with the right intention and direction, with the right state of mind when facing difficult challenges, and with the qualities of loving-kindness and compassion.

Follow your practice with easeful discipline and dedication

Because you need to gain a certain level of clarity to come to this point on the path, and because the path itself can at times be difficult to tread, you need to proceed with both dedication and easeful discipline.

Dedication is necessary because a certain level of consistency and strength is necessary for your practice to be effective and easeful discipline because it's important to travel the path with a sense of easefulness and joy. No matter how far along the path you are, your practice should be easeful and bring you great joy, not feel like a difficult trudge through the forest mud.

We'll talk at length about this in the next section, Part II: *Living Intentionally.*

Be open

So far, I've touched on the importance of being open and willing to accept whatever may come during your mindfulness practice, but it's so important that I feel the need to repeat it. You never know what you'll be presented with, so it can be easier said than done, but the effort needs to be there. It will make all the difference. Remember that this path you are on is the path to making friends with yourself and that you're not your own enemy, but someone longing to be a close friend.

We'll talk at length about this in Part III: *Living Naturally.*

Be kind to yourself through the process

Becoming your own best friend is not just about learning about ourselves intimately, but also learning to treat ourselves differently. To tread this path skillfully, it's imperative that you shift from breaking yourself down with criticism to bringing yourself up with loving-kindness and compassion. If this isn't done, you won't get very far along the path.

We'll talk at length about this in Part IV: *Living Lovingly.*

This Moment

To end this chapter, I'd like to tell a story which illustrates what it actually looks like to navigate this internal dialogue in everyday life. All this talk is nice and helpful, but without a direct example of what this looks like in actual application it's difficult to understand it clearly. This is a story about my *shoes*, but about so much more.

Facing the Internal Dialogue

The fear of what others think of you. It's one of the most pervading challenges we'll deal with in our entire life. Why is it such a difficult challenge? Because it seeps into almost everything we do, each and every day. I find it funny that we feel most free, most liberated, when we're doing things in a way that we don't care about what others think of us or what we're doing. But the pull to care what others think of us is so strong that even after experiencing a liberating experience such as that, we continue to be held in its vice.

One of the first projects I worked on when starting Buddhaimonia was a series on the top regrets of the dying. There was a story floating around the internet at the time about a woman by the name of Bronnie Ware and a book she wrote about her time working as a hospice nurse. During her time, she essentially interviewed her patients and asked them what their biggest regrets were. Surprisingly, they all said about the same five or so things. However, I wanted to take it further, so I took those regrets and looked for the recurring themes, to find out what they essentially all boiled down to. Do you know what was essentially the one major regret? It was:

Living in a way that the person cared (or cared too much) what other people thought of them and their actions.

We'll come back to that in a moment. First, the shoes...

The Shoes

About a year ago, I got a new pair of Toms. I love Toms, I love the style and appreciate what the company stands for. I've worn them for the past couple of years, but unfortunately I have a penchant for tearing mine up in a short period of time. My old ones were pretty torn up, especially the toe area (probably due to me being barefoot most of the time- I rarely wear socks). Well, as time went on, that fresh and beautiful new pair of Toms began to ware as well. My new pair has now gone through *much* more than the last. However, this isn't a story about my shoes. This is a story about what I realized as I continued to wear my shoes and as they became more and more torn up.

As time went on, I began noticing that I felt uncomfortable putting them on when I was getting dressed up to go somewhere public, particularly when it was a busy place like a mall or gathering with friends. After some time, it hit me- I was worried about what others would think of me.

Wow. They must not have any money.
Really...are you poor?
Dirty.
Trashy.
How sad.

These are all the things that I realized ran through my head as a part of wearing my shoes out in public places (not always, but often). Most of us would absolutely hate to admit it (it's not easy for me to write about it), but we don't like being thought of as these things. And that's perfectly OK, the majority of us were brought up to think these things were bad and to do whatever we had to to either avoid them or change our situation so that we weren't them. It's not our fault we turned out thinking that way.

For most of us, this is a part of our negative self-talk. A very critical part. One of the difficult parts about dealing with it is it's so subtle. My old pair was beaten up, and I felt the same way at times, but it never hit me. I never noticed it, but I *always* felt it- waking up can take time.

The Meditation

After gaining some clarity about the situation over the past year, noticing more and more how I felt when I put the shoes on to go out, I decided to make it into a little exercise, or meditation if you will. I decided to continue wearing my shoes- as confidently and proudly as ever- and to simply become mindful of the various thoughts and feelings that would arise in me. This was different from other mindfulness practices though, because I wasn't just observing. There was a special effect which happened as a result of me becoming aware of these thoughts and feelings in this way: I began sanding away at my ego.

I began to notice that each time I'd wear my shoes out to a busy location, thoughts and feelings would fly at me from time to time (at this point my mindfulness practice had magnified my ability to notice them, so they felt much stronger). And each time I'd recognize them with my mindfulness, I'd experience that uncomfortable feeling of having to face up to a part of my negative self-talk.

As time went on, and I continued to practice in this way, I felt as though my ego was shedding away, at least to some small degree. I was almost always uncomfortable, and I rarely liked the thoughts and feelings that arose, but over time it did become easier to handle. And after a few months, I began to feel quite liberated. I felt proud of my shoes and happy with myself in my own skin (more so than ever).

This Moment

Thoughts still came up from time to time, and I still felt the sting occasionally, but the change was quite noticeable.

And you know what else I realized?

No one cared.

No one ever cared about my shoes.

No one ever thought anything about them.

No one ever even noticed them.

They were all too busy worrying about themselves. We're all too busy worrying about ourselves. Every day that we step out and live our lives in a way that we care about what others think of us, it's just an exercise of the ego flexing its muscle over us.

These people I passed by in malls, stores, and gatherings didn't think those thoughts about me- *I thought those thoughts about me.* It was all ego. However, if we can have the courage to allow ourselves to be uncomfortable and face this internal dialogue, then we can begin to realize a great sense of liberation.

1. Accept that you have to get uncomfortable
2. Have courage
3. Be mindful
4. ...and be kind & compassionate with yourself

All it takes is little steps forward. Each day we're faced with tiny challenges. And it's by facing these challenges and making our way one step at a time that we make progress. The internal dialogue is sly and difficult to detect, but with mindfulness as our guiding light, we can make our way.

This Moment

Part II: Living Intentionally

This Moment

This Moment

What is the most important thing in this moment?

In Part I: *Living Mindfully,* we established the proper foundation of mindful living. However, as I mentioned earlier, this isn't enough. Consider for a moment living your life amid myriad distractions, consuming and associating with harmful nutriments, with misguided priorities, and living and practicing in a way that is hard and strenuous as opposed to easeful and joy-filled. You may not fall into all of those categories, but many of us fall into all or most, and to attempt to have a healthy mindful living practice, and find greater peace and happiness, amid these various factors is largely ineffective. Not only do these various factors get in the way of your mindfulness and meditative practice, but they harm your mental (and physical) well-being considerably.

Living intentionally is about living on purpose. In this case, in a very specific way. It's about the intentional effort to create an environment more conducive to peace, happiness, and freedom than the life you're living now. To live intentionally means you design your life: your surroundings, responsibilities, daily actions, and the quality of your effort in each moment. Specifically, we'll be working to:

1. Define a framework for peace, freedom, and overall greater well-being

2. Consume more mindfully through your various senses and better monitor the wholesome and unwholesome seeds in your mind
3. Improve focus and analyze your priorities, living with a one-pointed mind
4. Simplify daily life so as to cut down on distractions and mental clutter of all kinds
5. Improve the quality of your effort in daily life and practice and design a more effective environment for daily practice

But first, forget all that. Forget all of it. What's the most important thing in this moment? Before we venture off in these numerous directions and work on improving the quality of your day-to-day life through intentional living, it's important to understand the basic underlying idea behind the overall effort. And that's this:

What is the most important thing in this moment?

Throughout this part of the book this will be the guiding principle. When you distill living intentionally down to its essence, what do you get? Living in a way that you move away from what is harmful or unwholesome and towards that which is wholesome and nourishing with the purpose of promoting your well-being. That's the general idea. But to do this, we need a certain level of clarity. How can we create this environment of greater freedom if we don't even know where to go? The phrase "What is the most important thing in this moment?" gives us clarity and puts things in perspective in each moment of our life. It serves as a valuable guide in our effort towards living more intentionally and promoting our practice of mindful living. In many ways, living more fully and freely in the present moment is about considering what is the most important thing in this very moment over and over again.

This Moment

Keep in mind, that doesn't just have to be one thing. Or, at least, it doesn't usually pan out so simply. This is how the exercise usually goes for me:

What's the most important thing in this moment?

Be mindful.

What's the most important thing now?

[Realization] You know what, I really need to eat / do something else to take care of myself physically / mentally (eating is a good example for me because, well, I tend to forget to eat).

What's the most important thing now?

[Focus] I need to write (or whatever my top priority is for that day/moment).

Your first answer to the question will almost always be to become mindful. The question itself essentially compels you to become mindful, so it's just as much a natural byproduct as it is an answer to the question itself. After that, if you have the tendency to push yourself/rush around/become distracted like I do from time to time, you'll first realize you're being mindless and then next realize the state of your body such as your breathing, any aches in your body, hunger, or anything else, so the question is useful in helping you take care of yourself on multiple levels from moment-to-moment if you lead a relatively busy lifestyle. Lastly, you'll move on to the more obvious answer of what is the most important action to take with regards to your life as a whole. Each of these layers has to do with intentional living, but the third answer is really what we're getting at here.

This Moment

When you ask yourself, "what is the most important action, the most important thing I should be doing in this moment of my life?", you cut through the fluff. You cut through the distractions, the busyness, the mindlessness, and bring light to your life in that moment. If I'm distracted, doing something less important, or partaking in something that doesn't put my mental well-being first, I catch myself and can bring myself back to center. It's a simple question, but one which has profound use in daily life.

4-Fold Path of Peace

Imagine yourself tending to seeds in a garden.

      Because Part II: *Living Intentionally* is about establishing the proper environment in your daily life, it can be helpful to have a basic framework for your efforts. This basic framework is the 4-Fold Path of Peace. Of all the Buddha's teachings, the most fundamental is the 4 Noble Truths. The 4 Noble Truths outline the fundamental path out of suffering and to freedom, the path to arriving where we're all trying to go (whether we realize it or not). Within the 4 Noble Truths exists the 8-Fold Path, the basic framework for the 4th Noble Truth, which is the way to peace and happiness. The 8-Fold Path is an incredibly wise teaching and one which can serve anyone, whether they consider themselves Buddhist or not. However, I've always found that it's easier and therefore very helpful to think about the basic efforts behind the 8-Fold Path in a general sense, particularly in the beginning.

      Keep in mind, I'm in no way trying to step on the Buddha's feet here. For those looking for a more in-depth spiritual teaching, one which is steeped in a lifetime of wisdom, the Buddha's fundamental teachings are my highest suggestion. However, those looking for a basic framework for well-being and intentional living can easily become overwhelmed with these principles, which have great depth and are generally filled with language and principles completely foreign to most people. For that reason, the 4-Fold

This Moment

Path of Peace is a helpful framework which simplifies the general effort of improving your overall well-being and which is particularly useful for living more intentionally. It's ability to show us clearly how we can live more intentionally, due to the way it breaks our life down into sections, is why I mention it here.

The 4-Fold Path of Peace describes the four major areas of focus within creating this ideal environment conducive to greater peace and happiness and the ability to live more fully and freely in the present moment and helps guide you in your daily life by being able to monitor these fundamental areas. Imagine yourself tending to seeds in a garden. There are various areas of this garden and various different types of seeds. These areas are each of the four areas to the 4-Fold Path and the seeds are various wholesome and unwholesome seeds within our consciousness, the same seeds we seek to manage in the practice of living intentionally.

It's at this point that I feel it important to mention something. It's in this section of the book, more than any other, that some topics will venture into what might seem like unrelated territory. Simplifying your finances, for example. Don't become confused and think the book has become unfocused, though. This is all intentional (see what I did there?). Every area of this garden, and every piece of *Living Intentionally,* goes back to the same thing: cultivating an environment in your daily life more conducive to peace, happiness, and freedom. But to do that effectively, we can't leave out a single part of our lives.

So, going back to this garden. This is the metaphor I'll use time and time again in this part of the book because I feel it's most effective at allowing you to visualize the proper effort that needs to be made. In many ways, the 4-Fold Path of Peace shadows the major principles of *This Moment* in each of its four sections. Also, keep in mind, I use the word "Clear" as the first word of each section's title to notate the clearing of the pathway to peace and freedom, the overall intention. Let's dive in to each individual area of this garden now.

1. *Clear Understanding + Purpose*
2. *Clear Mind-Body*
3. *Clear Inter-Mind-Body*
4. *Clear Practice*

Clear Understanding + Purpose

Clear Understanding means understanding the basic principles of the path to peace and freedom. To give you a clear example of what I mean, *This Moment* itself is one large effort to transmit a clearer understanding to you, so there isn't much else to mention here. Included within this can also be additional teachings or teachers which you've deemed important through your life experiences and any ongoing additional learning towards that same purpose.

Clear Purpose refers to having clear motivation and intentions:

What led you to practice?
Why do you practice now?
Why don't you practice?
What pulls you away from your practice?

Your purpose, why you take action in any given moment (or why you don't), and learning how to cultivate a wholesome one, is a fundamental factor in successfully following a daily practice such as the one outlined in *This Moment*.

Someone with Clear Understanding + Purpose has a firm grasp of the path and not only is aware of their motivating factors but is in control of them as well. Clear

Understanding + Purpose deals most notably with Part III: *Living Naturally* as well as Part II to some degree.

Clear Mind-Body

Clear Mind-Body is about properly nourishing the mind-body. Keep in mind, when I say mind-body I do so intentionally to refer to the mind and body as one inseparable entity. It's a mistake to think of the mind and body as separate and for good reason. The mind and body are connected in countless ways, many of which have significance with regards to our well-being. One great example is pain. Pain is a result of the nervous system, of which the brain is essentially in control of. However, we tend to think of pain as being solely a part of the physical body. Of course, physical pain is felt in the physical body, but we can't make such straight assumptions without looking more closely into a subject. With mindfulness practice, we can change the way we relate with pain because of this brain-nervous system connection, so we need to be aware of the connected nature of mind and body.

A healthy mind-body deals with a number of categories, all of which we'll go into detail on in this part of the book:

- People-based associations
- Mental food
- Physical food
- Anything else placed into the body from one of the six sense organs
- Plus, intentional actions that harm the mind-body

Someone with Clear Mind-Body is not only aware of the garden of consciousness, something we'll talk about in the next chapter, but they have worked diligently to clear away, or at least lower the presence of, unwholesome (harmful) seeds and promote wholesome seeds throughout their life. Clear

Mind-Body deals most notably with this part of the book (Part II), particularly next chapter.

Clear Inter-Mind-Body

Clear Inter-Mind-Body is about properly nourishing the mind-body connection between you and those you connect with.

- Mindful communication
- Cultivating understanding and compassion
- Practicing true love (compassion, joy, loving-kindness, freedom/equanimity)
- The Buddha's Right Livelihood

Someone with Clear Inter-Mind-Body is not only aware of the direct connection between their own well-being and the well-being of others, they've worked diligently to cultivate healthy connections between themselves and other beings in major areas. Clear Inter-Mind-Body deals most notably with Part IV: *Living Lovingly.*

Clear Practice

Clear Practice is about putting into practice Clear Understanding. It's about dedicating oneself to obtaining freedom, the freedom to live more fully and freely in the present moment.

Living mindfully, which we covered in detail in Part I, is a big part of Clear Practice. But this point deals very much with each of the other three parts of *This Moment* as well, specifically the actual practice-oriented material.

Someone with Clear Practice not only has the intention to practice in a diligent and dedicated way, but they've worked to develop that practice and make it strong and healthy. Clear Practice deals most notably with Part I: *Living Mindfully*, but it deals with the other three parts of the book in a number of ways as well.

Now that we've covered each of the four areas, understand that monitoring the areas of the 4-Fold Path of Pcacc is a simple process of reviewing each of the areas to see if you're healthy in each. Imagine yourself walking through the various areas of this garden. You check to see if each of the areas is getting enough water, enough sunlight, and making sure none of the plants are growing on top of one another and have enough room to grow. If not, you make the necessary adjustments to ensure each area of the garden continues to be healthy.

For each area, it can be the simple practice of asking yourself, "am I healthy in this area?" Is there something you're confused about, something you don't understand? Maybe there's something you can do to improve in Clear Understanding. Then again, maybe there isn't. Some things just have to unfold on their own. Is your practice less consistent than you'd like it to be? Are you lacking self-love or compassion? Maybe you need to place more focus on your daily practice in that area. Often, simply asking the question, "am I healthy in this area?", is enough to know if you're lacking in any of the areas. Intuitively, we often know what to do to improve the situation without having to do any searching.

Keep in mind, each of these four areas overlap and intersect in many ways, so it's not so cut-and-dry. But the 4-Fold Path of Peace can serve as a valuable guide on the journey to clearing away the "fog", living more intentionally, and with greater peace and freedom.

Mindful Consumption and the Garden of Consciousness

"Man is what he eats."

- German proverb

In the last chapter, we spoke about the four areas of the 4-Fold Path of Peace as being akin to a garden which we must attend to. In this chapter, we'll continue to discuss the garden of our mind, now looking a little closer into the factors that affect these seeds and the actual tending to the seeds which grow within this garden through the practice of mindful consumption.

Once again, imagine that your mind is like a garden and that within this garden exist seeds. Each of these seeds is a mental formation. Anger, joy, fear, frustration, jealousy, compassion, loving-kindness, and on and on. Every feeling or mental quality has its own respective seed. Each seed within your consciousness has been given a certain level of attention over the span of your life. For instance, fear may have sprouted and become a prominent flower because you've developed the habit of worrying due to being conditioned by various life experiences. Maybe anger and frustration is a growing seed within your store consciousness (think the basement of your consciousness, where the potential for all things and all mental formations exists) because the circumstances of a recent tragedy have left you blaming yourself. Throughout your mind, some seeds are full-grown, others have just sprouted, and others are nothing more than potential seeds within your store consciousness. Each of these seeds, when sprouted, plays a part in affecting the quality of your life. And, more often than not, we've unfortunately watered far more harmful seeds than we have wholesome ones and this significantly affects our well-being. This is the garden of our consciousness and this is where the work of mindful consumption lies.

Interconnectivity and Mindful Consumption

So far, we've discussed the garden of our consciousness and the importance of tending to it. This is, in large part, the practice of mindful consumption. Mindful consumption is about consuming in a way that we promote wholesome seeds and discourage unwholesome ones. A critical point about mindful consumption is the understanding of interconnectedness and the effect outside forces have on us (and also our effect on outside forces).

Mindful consumption is about waking up. It's about being more keenly aware of what you consume with your senses (including the mind) and of the effect those things have on you. It's about appreciating yourself as well as everything around you through seeing and acting with greater clarity. It goes beyond the traditional understanding of self-development, clears up the illusory and confusing separation between self-development and spirituality and introduces the concept of you not as a separate person but as interconnected to all other people and things. To understand what I mean by that and to know how you should

This Moment

approach mindful consumption, I need to explain something first.

As living beings, we're much more like plants than we tend to realize. Depending on how much sun, water and other nutrients you absorb you'll either grow or wilt. Of course, the nutrients we need are different than what a plant needs, but it works in much the same way. You need to absorb various nutrients on a regular basis. You can't just do it every once in a while and you can't just get water with no sunlight. You need to cover some rough combination of certain critical ingredients to properly nourish yourself- to perform at your best and to be your happiest, healthiest and most energetic self.

When practicing mindfulness, we touch the world around us deeply. This can bring us great happiness. But there's more to it than just the ability to more deeply experience and appreciate the world around us. When practicing mindfulness, we also see very deeply into the things with which we're interacting with, which is the reason mindfulness, when paired with concentration, is the basis for insight. Through the practice of developing mindfulness and concentration, we can receive insight and see into the true nature of things.

Take an orange for example. While mindfully eating an orange we may see, or realize, that the orange is made up of completely non-orange elements. We see the orange tree with which the orange came from. We see the rain water that helped the orange tree, and therefore the orange, grow. Because of the rain we see the clouds, we also see the sun and the soil from which the orange tree grew from. You can see the farmer that grew the orange and you can also see the pesticides it was treated with along the way, among other things. So you see that the orange is made up of many different things. Everything affects the orange or contributes to its growth or death and the orange will then go on to do the same to everything that it touches, including us.

This Moment

In The Art of Power, Thich Nhat Hanh explains:

Everything is related *to everything else. Your well-being and the well-being of your family are essential elements in bringing about the well-being of your business or of any organization where you work. Finding ways to protect yourself and promote your own well-being is the most basic investment you can make. This will have an impact on your family and work environment, but* first of all *it will result in an improvement in* the quality of *your own life.*

This is the very basis of mindful consumption. And you don't have to receive any sort of special insight to see this. By simply becoming aware of the interconnected nature of all things you'll begin to see the effect other things have on you and the effect you have on other things. You can then make a more conscious choice to consume more of the things that feed your mind and body in a wholesome way, whether it's a certain type of food, a TV show or some sort of relationship, or reduce or even eliminate your consumption of those things that feed you mind and body in an unwholesome way. This is what mindful consumption looks like in application.

Mindful consumption has two steps:

1. Awareness

That is, becoming fully aware of the complete effect that all things consumed by your senses have on your well-being and on the world around you.

2. Consumption

Next, consuming wisely based on that knowledge: eliminating, reducing and avoiding those things which don't

This Moment

serve you and the world around you and adding and promoting those things which do.

Mindful consumption includes a huge variety of things. Really, it has to do with everything you do every single day. Also, mindful consumption includes a number of things you might not yet have associated with having an affect on your well-being. It includes not only the obvious things such as what we eat and drink but also what we watch, read and listen to. All of these things affect you in various different ways.

One last note about mindful consumption: it doesn't mean simply feed yourself good things and avoid the bad. Mindful consumption is about looking deeply into everything that you do, as I mentioned earlier, and really seeing into the true nature of things. It's about getting the complete and fully educated picture. Then, using that insight to make the conscious decision to consume more or less of that thing based on the effect it has on you. Make no assumptions in mindful consumption and allow the clear vision that your mindfulness and meditative practice cultivates in you to guide you. Don't just eat more vegetables because other people tell you to, really do your research and look into why you should eat vegetables. What do the various vitamins and minerals do that exist in each vegetable? What's the best way to consume them? Why is proper nutrition important? You only have so many hours in a day and a finite amount of mental energy, is that really a priority? Mindful consumption is about making conscious decisions, not just taking conventional wisdom at face value.

As you can see, mindful consumption runs deeper than "this is good, I should do it". More important than taking on wholesome things and discouraging the unwholesome is focusing on the areas with which we can consume and working on becoming healthier in each area (or maintaining the area if you are healthy in it). By doing this, you'll have a much easier time practicing mindful consumption in both an easeful and effective way.

The practice of mindful consumption is available to everyone and in every moment and should be practiced diligently if we ever hope to live fully and freely in the present moment. The reality is that neither you nor I have the ability to avoid being affected by these various factors (everything which touches our senses), no matter how strong we think we are. Everything around us, especially those things we consume regularly, affect us and in a very concrete way. You need to take steps to discourage the growth of unwholesome seeds in your life and to water the wholesome ones.

Unfortunately, many of us are closer to the other side of the spectrum. We live mindlessly and unconsciously. We talk about people behind their backs negatively, complain about our day at work when we're home or about home when we're at work. We watch reality shows filled with nothing but people fighting and insulting one another for entertainment. We read articles and blogs about Hollywood drama and partake in bashing our politicians and government officials instead of trying to create that positive change ourselves.

Buddhist wisdom, particularly the monastic way as a monk or nun, emphasizes simplifying one's life and mindful consumption. What this means in Buddhist terms is to weed out distractions and negative influences, such as the ones I just mentioned, which can make it difficult to follow the way to greater awakening. However, this stands true no matter what you believe or practice. Until you weed out these distractions and negative influences you can never hope to find true peace or happiness.

Right Effort

Living intentionally is ultimately about cultivating the right effort. It's about improving the quality of your life in each moment through improving the quality of your effort. In each moment, are you touching something wholesome, unwholesome, or neutral? And are you doing it in a wholesome or unwholesome way? This effort is what the Buddha referred to as Right Effort (or Right Diligence) in his 8-Fold Path, and he established a helpful 4-point guideline for understanding it called 4-Fold Right Diligence:

4-Fold Right Diligence

1. Preventing unwholesome seeds in our store consciousness which have not yet arisen from arising.
2. Helping the unwholesome seeds which have already arisen to go back to our store consciousness.
3. Finding ways to water the wholesome seeds in our store consciousness that have not yet arisen.
4. Nourishing the wholesome seeds that have already arisen so that they will stay present and grow stronger.

Those four points perfectly sum up the overall effort of this chapter and the practice of mindful consumption. Tending to the garden of the mind by consuming mindfully is about cleansing the mind of harmful influences (or at least not placing additional attention on them) and placing the proper attention on wholesome ones. In this way, you can "clear the pathway" so to speak, therein creating an environment more conducive to peace, happiness, and freedom. It's in this proper balance of watering wholesome seeds and managing unwholesome ones that we can create this environment of peace I spoke about in the beginning of Part II.

Keep in mind, mindful consumption is a life-long effort. Your work is never truly done. Store consciousness in Buddhist psychology represents a sort of potentiality. There's always the potential for anger, fear, hatred, joy, excitement, and peace but they're not always apparent because the seeds aren't always being watered. Or, in other words, our actions aren't creating the conditions for them to arise. It's important to remember this as you go about your life, not only because it means you always hold the potential for love and joy within you when things appear dark (wholesome seeds can always sprout again), but also because it means you always hold the potential for fear, anger, and attachment in you as well (unwholesome seeds are never truly gone). This is why mindful consumption is a daily practice, a life-long effort for promoting your well-being.

Living intentionally is ultimately about cultivating the right effort. It's about improving the quality of your life in each moment through improving the quality of your effort.

Primary Seeds

I've touched on a few examples of the difference seeds that exist within us, but let's quickly cover the major seeds so that you have a clearer understanding when we talk about mindful consumption. It's important to be able to identify these formations when they arise in our mind so that we can handle them skillfully.

Unwholesome seeds include:

- *Fear*
- *Anger*
- *Greed*
- *Jealousy*
- *Ignorance*
- *Wrong views*

These are just some of the many unwholesome seeds that exist within us. Unwholesome seeds include fear, anger, and greed, three of the major unwholesome seeds to watch out for. Included within here can also be regret, disappointment, sorrow, hatred, and so many others.

Wholesome seeds include:

- *Compassion*
- *Loving-kindness*
- *Joy*
- *Peace*
- *Equanimity*
- *Calmness / Tranquility*

And these are just some of the major wholesome seeds. Other wholesome seeds can be respect/admiration, caring, and confidence. Seeds such as love and joy should be watered on a daily basis. This is a big part of our daily practice.

How to Practice: Mindful Consumption

So far, we've talked about what mindful consumption is and the garden of our consciousness, but we haven't talked about exactly how we can consume more mindfully, more skillfully. The basic idea behind mindful consumption, the primary effort, is to become aware of:

1. *The quality of a thing: is it harmful? Is it wholesome? Is it not so black-and-white?*
2. *How much attention we're putting into a given thing.*
3. *What we need to do to change the situation, either by better promoting a wholesome seed or*

discouraging an unwholesome one. Review your options and decide on the best course of action.

Once we have this information- and we get this by paying close attention to our lives with our mindfulness practice- it's about simply taking action, paying attention to what happens as a result, and making adjustments as necessary. I call this mindful consumption, as opposed to something like conscious living (a term I've used before), because it's our mindfulness practice which is the guiding light in unearthing the three points of information we need to take action that I listed above, as opposed to just listening to conventional wisdom (which isn't always very wise) as I mentioned earlier. Mindfulness plays a big part in allowing us to consume and act more skillfully in this way, so I feel that mindful consumption is more fitting.

In this section, we'll cover the major areas for consuming mindfully. Ultimately, mindful consumption comes down to the concept of different types of food, also called nutriment. Specifically, physical and mental food:

Physical Food

1. *Eating*
2. *Drinking*
3. *Healing and Medicating*

Mental Food

4. *Purchasing*
5. *Watching*
6. *Reading*
7. *Associating*

Physical Food

In this first section, Physical Food, I'm going to cover mindful physical consumption for the sake of improving the condition of your body on a day-to-day basis. This is all about *maintaining your energy levels and helping you feel more alert.* Overall, just making your body *feel* better on a day-to-day basis, something a proper diet can help with quite a bit.

What I won't talk about is consuming mindfully for weight loss or to reduce your risk of major diseases (i.e. the typical reasons people think of for eating healthy). It's your choice whether or not those are important things to you. For the sake of the topic at hand, though, cultivating a mind, practice, and overall environment which allows us to live more fully and freely in the present moment, those hold little value.

Listed below are the major areas of mindful consumption. These are the things you should become more aware of in your everyday life and educate yourself on to make your own decisions based on your life- your needs and preferences. Keep in mind that mostly the same things apply for all of us, but there are exceptions. Remember not to take anything at face value and apply it to your own life. Examine your life closely and make a more aware decision.

Lastly, don't worry about being perfect. Perfection is just an idea, it doesn't exist in the real world and hanging on to an idea of perfection won't help you. Like all other efforts that have to do with improving your life, it takes time and you'll invariably get some things wrong at first. Just make your best effort and you'll quickly see the change that living more consciously has on our lives. Lastly, I know each point is pretty big, so I'd suggest picking two of these points at a time that go well together (mindful eating and drinking for instance) and working on those first. Later, you can come back and work on another group.

1. Eating

Mindful consumption of food is about knowing how the food you put into your body will affect you. By becoming more aware of the way you consume food, as well as of the effect the food you put into your body will have on you, not only will your eating patterns become healthier, but by being careful of what you put into your body you can increase your energy levels substantially.

Remember the orange? In the same way that countless factors affected the orange's growth, development, and even its existence, so does everything affect us. Food, in particular, plays a large role in each of those areas. The two major things to pay attention to with mindful consumption of physical food, are:

1. *What* you put into your body
2. *How (and why)* you put food into your body

With regards to what you put into your body, on one end there's being mindful of the way it affects your body, specifically how you feel on a day-to-day basis and your general energy or vitality levels. The general suggestions are less fast-food, sugary drinks, and foods lacking real nutrition and more whole foods and water. On the other end, moving outward, it's about being aware of how what you eat affects your loved ones and the rest of the world. Now, that might seem like I'm veering off. But, as you'll learn particularly in Part IV, it's actually ignoring the well-being of others which is veering off the path to true peace and happiness. Your well-being and the well-being of your loved ones is directly connected in numerous ways, many of which are often too difficult to see at first. At least, until you look more closely.

This Moment

Consider, for a moment, that what you eat influences what your immediate family eats. In fact, everything you do affects everyone around you. Maybe it's a little difficult to see right now why you should take such a vested interest in others so far away from you. I understand completely. We're so far away from them, and therefore find it difficult to garner a real emotional connection. However, when using the example of an immediate loved one, we can clearly begin to see just how important the other end of mindful consumption is. Now, this is easy to see. If you eat more McDonalds, is your family more likely to eat McDonalds? Of course they are, even if it's a subtle change (which it probably wouldn't be). If you buy healthier snacks and, of course, keep them in the fridge and cabinets of your home, are your immediate family members more likely to eat healthier? It's not hard to imagine that they would, especially due to human curiosity. Then, consider the fact that this comes back around to you and affects your ability to consistently eat healthy. That's just one example, but you get the idea.

Second, with regards to how and why you put food into your body, I'm really talking about eating disorders. You already know that mindfulness practice allows us to identify harmful patterns of behavior, but this doesn't stop with mental activity. It also extends beyond to our physical actions. The National Eating Disorder Association reports that 10-15% of all Americans suffer from some type of serious eating disorder.[4] That's a huge percentage of people being affected by real eating disorders, not just, "I can't put down this chocolate" (which isn't meant to poke fun, but rather illustrate a distinction). Now, I'm no eating disorder specialist, but I do know the power of mindfulness practice and mindful consumption of eating for eating disorders. When we pay close attention to our actions with mindfulness practice, we eventually uncover the "root" of the action: i.e. why we do it. Once this happens, we have the opportunity to take a wholesome action to begin working through that challenge.

And this is what mindful consumption of food with regards to how and why we consume food is about.

2. Drinking

What you put into your body really does make a difference. In fact, some of the most significant improvements to your health and vitality can be made via changing what you drink. There's a few beverages worth mentioning, namely: water, soda/juice, and alcohol. Of all those, water is critically important for your body and plays a noticeable role in your daily energy levels, something I've tested thoroughly over the years.

I've followed Mercola.com for most of my health related advice for some time now. I've followed a lot of websites for health advice and few have been as helpful and thorough as Dr. Mercola's website. He had this to say in his article "The Case Against Drinking 6-8 Glasses of Water a Day":

It is my strong belief that the single most powerful intervention the majority of Americans can make for their physical health would be to stop drinking all sodas and juices and replace them with health promoting pure water.

He goes on to say that:

If you get the fluid/water replacement issue right, then you have made one of the most important and powerful steps you can in taking control of your health.

Lastly, alcohol. Even casual drinking over the course of years can damage your brain and it does you no real good. Not to mention, you or someone you care about and spend time with could have the potential for alcoholism and not even know it, which could lead to much worse things. You'll find that with a healthy spiritual practice intoxicating yourself for a little fun stops being so attractive. You'll realize the only reason you ever did it was either out of peer pressure or to temporarily numb some sort of internal pain.

As suggested above, the primary suggestion here is to reduce consumption of sugary drinks and alcohol and replace with water. There are some exceptions I feel, though. Coconut water, for instance, is a great replacement for sugary drinks as it has a lot of health benefits, hydrates the body well like water, and has a lot of electrolytes which contribute to your body's energy levels. Keep in mind, though, that any suggestions I make throughout these sections are just general bits of advice. As I mentioned earlier, our lives are far too varied for me to give specific advice that applies to even a majority of people. Only you can make those decisions. The most important thing is that you have a framework to base your efforts off of. And, also, it's about paying attention to *your body*, not about taking my advice and applying it to your body blindly. That's the most important point of all.

3. Healing and Medicating

Healing might not seem like something that would be associated with mindful consumption, but when you consider that the majority of us rush to consume either over-the-counter or prescription drugs anytime something is remotely wrong with us then you'll see that how you react to pain and illness (whether minor or major) is an important part of this section.

In The Art of Power, Thich Nhat Hanh speaks about how we've forgotten our bodies natural healing ability:

When an animal in the forest gets seriously wounded, it knows exactly what to do. It looks for a secluded spot and just lies down for several days, not concerned with eating. It has wisdom. Only when the wound has healed does the animal return to foraging or hunting for food.

We once had this kind of wisdom, but now we have lost our capacity to rest. We panic every time we experience something uncomfortable in our body. We rush to the doctor to get a prescription for all kinds of medicine because we don't realize that just allowing our body to rest is often the best method of healing.

"Thay", as his students lovingly refer to him as (pronounced 'tie'), suggests using mindfulness to speed up the healing process as opposed to depending so heavily on medication. How do you practice mindful healing? Mindful healing is simply mindfulness of the body in a concentrated setting (i.e. as a formal mindfulness practice):

How to Practice: Mindfulness of Body

To practice mindfulness of body, you can focus your complete awareness on the affected area or on your entire body as a whole.

1. Find a comfortable place to lie down

This is a formal practice, so preferably find somewhere you can concentrate more easily. This could be your bed, but keep in mind that this exercise is liable to put you to sleep, so the floor may be a better option to maintain alertness.

2. Scan the body with mindfulness

To practice mindfulness of the entire body, start with your head and stay in mindfulness as you go slowly through each area of your body. Concentrate on each individual area of the body for a few moments.

3. Place extra focus on problem areas

When you get to an area of your body causing you trouble, take a few extra moments and give extra attention to that area. Take a few purposely deep breaths while you continue focusing on the area.

Unfortunately, most people, at least in the U.S., choose drugs over natural healing. There's a lot of different over-the-counter and prescription drugs out there and the number is growing every day. I'm sure you've seen the commercials where it's the same beautifully perfect day in every single commercial followed by what sounds like an insane list of side effects. Drug companies bring in billions of dollars every year, and with money, comes greed. I'm not saying everyone associated with a big pharmaceutical company has fallen to greed and every medication a cash-pull. However, I am saying that the cases are prevalent enough that you need to be careful and educate yourself about what medication you consume and really ask yourself:

1. *Do I need it? And...*
2. *Is there a more natural alternative?*

Do your research, be aware of all the possibilities, stay mindful of the signals your body is sending you, introduce yourself to natural healing remedies, and practice mindful healing. It's in your hands to be mindful and to make a more educated and ultimately aware choice.

Mental Food

Mental food is when we get into less-familiar territory. Remember that mindful consumption is anything that we consume with our senses, which includes our eyes and ears. Keep in mind, it also includes the mind, as I'll talk about a bit in this section. That one can be a bit tricky to understand.

Mental food deals with 4 major areas:

1. *Who you surround yourself with (Associations):* Who are the people you're around the most? Do any of those people water unwholesome seeds in you on a consistent basis? Should you distance yourself from those people?
2. *What you read:* Blogs, magazines, news, and books.
3. *What you watch:* Online videos (YouTube, etc.), T.V., movies.
4. *What you listen to:* Music, radio news & shows, podcasts, audiobooks, etc.

The general effort for each of these categories is to ask yourself:

1. *What do I consume on a regular basis? And...*
2. *Are these activities watering wholesome or unwholesome seeds in me?*

4. Purchasing

If mindful consumption is about being mindful of what you absorb through your senses, and we're talking about creating an environment more conducive to peace and freedom, then purchasing is an important point to consider because it effects many of the other categories here.

Mindful consumption of the things we buy is about being mindful of the impact which something you buy will have on you, on others, on the planet and of the purpose for which you're purchasing it. Because of the first reason, being mindful of the impact, everything else on this list is directly connected to this point in some way. The second reason I need to explain a bit further. Being mindful of the purpose for which you purchase something is about being mindful to not clutter your life with needless or useless things. This can eventually have a number of negative effects on you and those around you, so it's important to consider just for this one reason alone.

I'd suggest starting out here slowly. When you go to buy or acquire something just start by asking yourself these two questions:

1. *Do I really need this?*
2. *Will this positively or negatively affect me and/or others around me? Or both?*

This can be a whole lifestyle change in itself, so take it one step at a time and stay true yourself in the process. Keep in mind, this is a big subject, but we'll go into it in more detail in *Simplifying Your Life* within this part of the book.

5. Watching

By watching I'm referring exclusively to watching TV, movies and videos on the internet (you could include video games here, as well). This one is pretty straightforward.

This Moment

Things to be mindful of here are your total daily screen time (TV, phone, desktop, any other sort of screen), how many hours a day you're sitting and what kinds of things you're watching.

You probably already know that staring at a screen for long hours each day isn't exactly good for you, but more than ever you need to be mindful of how much screen time you're clocking every day because of how difficult it is to get away from them. This can not only affect your ability to focus, but your attention span as well. We use screens for everything from work to play nowadays. Chances are you need to cut down on your screen time. An easy exercise to do is to pay attention to how often you check your email and social accounts throughout your day and to cut each down to once or twice a day if possible. Really stop to think about the things you do on your phone especially those of which are just time wasters or unwholesome associations and seek to cut them off or minimize them. You probably work, or at least communicate, using your phone and desktop, though, and generally do nothing but waste time watching TV- so it's an easier target. If you're an avid screen watcher, do this experiment: cut your TV time by half or one-third and immediately start doing something positive with that time like reading a book or going for walks outside. See how you feel after one week. Pay close attention to your mood, energy level and ability to focus on whatever task is at hand during this period and for the weeks afterwards.

Second, be mindful of the effect that shows with not-so-good themes and advertisements can have on your state of mind. You need to pay close attention to this. If it doesn't feed your mind or contribute to anything wholesome it probably should be minimized or eliminated (all depending on your life and what it is). Now, I'm not telling you to stop watching your favorite show. You don't need to take it that far, but what I am saying is to become mindful of the effect that the things you consume have on you and simply to minimize the unwholesome.

As with every category here, take it slow. At first, you can just focus on the obvious things that contribute to watering unwholesome seeds and then move on gradually from there.

6. Reading

People love reading about gossip and drama. If they didn't, those magazines with all those bogus celebrity stories on the news stands of grocery stores wouldn't still be there decades after their inception. When they told you in elementary school that reading is good, they didn't mean stuff like that.

Mindful consumption of what you read means being mindful of the effect that whatever you're reading has on you and choosing those things that nourish your mind over those that don't. That means staying away from gossip, drama and most other unwholesome forms of writing be it a physical publication or a blog, magazine or news source online. It also means that when you do read it should be something that feeds your mind.

Keep in mind that you can't, and shouldn't, stay away from all negative news. I keep up with world news. I think it's important to do so. But man...it can be difficult at times. Read through one week's worth of headlines and your general enthusiasm for the world as a whole will usually drop a few points. But this is our world, the real world. And it's not all pretty. There's a lot of beauty, but there's a lot of chaos as well. It's important to know what's going on not just in a general sense but so that we can help our brothers and sisters in any way possible. If you live in the U.S. or another well-off nation you tend lead a sheltered life unaware of the hardships of other nations, so it's important to educate yourself. Also, in this way, the outer world reflects our internal world. We need to learn to become comfortable in our own skin- this is the process of making friends with ourselves- and that means facing the not-so-bright parts. For this reason, the practice of accepting the dark patches of the world and still holding love and compassion for it is an exercise that has merit for improving our own internal well-being.

Mindful consumption of what you read, and mindful consumption as a whole, isn't just about consuming good things. It's about seeing reality as it is. To see with clarity. That means, as we've spoken about throughout this section, that you realize the effect the things you consume have on you and can therefore make a more wholesome choice for the sake of your well-being and the well-being of the world around you.

7. Associating

Mindful consumption of who you associate with is about being careful about who you talk to and spend time with on a regular basis, both online and off. The people you associate, or communicate, with are the most powerful people in your life and some of the most powerful forces in your life period. I can't stress this enough. It's so important to keep company with positive, loving and compassionate people. It really does effect everything you do. By keeping as many positive associations and as few negative ones in your life, you'll be happier and more at peace. By being mindful of your associations you'll be able to decide which ones are and aren't positive associations.

OK, that sounds great. However, in real life, it can be much more difficult to be choosy about who you talk and spend time with. You might even live with someone who isn't the greatest association. This can be really difficult. Trust me, I know how it is. I've lived with people who were pretty bad associations as well. In these situations, you need to meditate on the person in hopes of cultivating compassion and understanding towards them otherwise you'll be bothered by them every day. Know that it's a deep-seated anger, resentment or ignorance being projected outward. Understand this and you can continue to show compassion towards them.

In addition, you don't want to hang around these people any longer than you have to. You can't change someone else for them, that person has to want to change themselves. And if they just don't want to change their ways, you need to get away. This isn't always possible, I understand. However, you can find more peace regardless. In fact, it's through these struggles that you will grow to appreciate your practice of mindful and intentional living even more. Ultimately, all that can be done is for you to do your best. This is part of your practice in itself. No matter what arises, accepting it fully with all of your being. It's about turning inward and discovering freedom from complete and radical acceptance.

The Most Important Thing

Wake up to your life in the present moment and realize that every small action makes waves like ripples in a pond.

Remember, mindful consumption includes your entire life, so it's a huge topic. Don't become overwhelmed with all the various different ways you can consume more mindfully and get confused about where to start first. Remember what is the most important thing: tend to the garden of the mind. To nourish the wholesome seeds in you and to do as few things that would water the unwholesome seeds. To live mindfully and to really take the time to educate yourself and become more alive to the world around you.

This Moment

Be aware of your interconnected nature (our interbeing) and of how one thing affects many things and how many things affect one thing. This is life, so by living your life in a way that you become more aware of this layered relationship you put yourself in a position to experience greater peace and happiness. However you choose to live your life, what's really important is that you consume more mindfully. Wake up to your life in the present moment and realize that every small action makes waves like ripples in a pond.

One-Pointed Mind

"Since there is never a time when worldly activities come to an end, limit your activities."

- Atisa

In meditative practice, it's concentration which is the defining characteristic that leads to awakening and the receiving of insight. Without this concentration factor, our meditation practice would be impossible. It's what unlocks numerous critical insights which helps us live more skillfully. In the same way, concentrating our overall efforts in daily life allows for a sort of "opening up".

By living in a way that we let our efforts and intentions be swayed by every little thing that passes by us, we end up ineffective at everything that we do. And before you think, "I just want to be happy. I don't want to be successful, or need a big house, etc.", in other words believing that you don't need to become effective at any particular effort in life to find peace and happiness, you're mistaken. Even the path to peace and freedom takes a specific type of effort. It takes dedication and diligence. There should be a sort of easefulness to the way you move about your life and practice, so I'm not necessarily talking about strenuous effort, but to think that you don't have to work hard at your practice is a misunderstanding. And so, knowing this, to go about it in an unfocused way is to create a needless hurdle for you to jump over each time you go to practice. In your daily life, this takes many shapes.

In daily life, various responsibilities are constantly pulling at us. There's work, finances, family, intimate relationships, kids, additional personal responsibilities, and of course let's not forget your daily mindfulness and meditation practice (and any other spiritual commitments and responsibilities you choose to partake in). To a large degree, you live your practice in every moment, but I consider it here because it's something which must still be remembered, prioritized and acted upon (plus, there is still a formal aspect to part of the practice). To be without clear priorities in your life is to put each and every one of those categories up to the wind and say, "here, land where you may." You'll always guide them to some degree, albeit maybe unconsciously, but without a clear sense of what is most important to you and how that will unfold in your life, to some degree you're placing your well-being up to the wind.

A Word on Intentions

At this point, you might be wondering how living with a one-pointed mind, prioritizing what's most important in your life and actively discouraging what is less or not important at all, can coincide with living freely and accepting whatever may come. This is why I titled Part II *Living Intentionally*. It's not titled *Manifesting Your Desires* or *Making Your Dreams Come True*, both titles suggesting a sort of forceful pushing to design your life in a specific way with deep expectations attached. And when that doesn't happen, the friction caused by that expectation not being met creates additional, once avoidable, suffering in you.

Living Intentionally connotes purposely doing something, so we are taking action, and that is important to some degree, but purposely doing something has no immediate connection to any expectation as opposed to something like *Manifesting Your Desires*. It's important to understand that living intentionally is about drawing a picture in the sand of what you believe, through your direct experience, the most wholesome and nourishing ingredients and direction are for your life in an effort to promote your well-being and practice of cultivating peace and freedom. Then, allowing the wind to do with it what it will. *Accepting that this is how things will go (how life is) is an essential part of living intentionally.*

Living with a One-Pointed Mind

You can only give your time and attention to so many things. Because we have a finite amount of time in this life and in each individual moment, you need to get to the heart of what's most important to you and give yourself fully to those things. As we spoke about earlier, to live in each moment, doing each thing, with all of your being, makes a significant and concrete difference in the quality of your day-to-day experience. With regards to living with a one-pointed mind, this involves:

1. *Deciding what's beneficial and most important to you.*
2. *Simplifying your life (cutting down on the nonessentials/distractions).*
3. *And giving yourself fully to those beneficial and important things.*

In a life filled with potential distractions and with the chance for surprises and pitfalls at every turn, it's only in doing this that you'll be able to live a life of no regrets. A life where you felt that you gave it your all in each moment. Simplifying your life and focusing your priorities may only be a container- the practice of mindful and harmonious living and cultivating love being the contents- but without the container, we'd have no effective capacity to create the right environment for peace and freedom to arise in the first place. This container, which protects and promotes our practice is, in yet another way, an essential part of living intentionally.

Deciding What's Most Important

Most of us are striving, or at least moving, towards something (or things). We have a dream or a goal and we want to achieve it, and we look forward to the way our life will be once we accomplish it. In many ways, having a dream and a goal is just fine. However, it's natural for us to become attached to it, to the point where we convince ourselves that we can't be happy until we get it. This is, of course, completely untrue. This kind of attachment is very unhealthy, and unfortunately it's something that most of us have fallen for (I was no exception).

This first step is very much about deciding what's most important to you in your life through the lens of understanding this form of attachment or unhealthy desire. It's important to go through the exercise of deciding what's most important to you from this lens, because if you neglect it you could run into a whole different problem. Instead of lacking focus and intention you'd be striving towards something in an unhealthy way, both routes that lead to additional challenges and the resulting suffering.

There are two primary questions here:

1. *What matters most to you? Why is it important to you?* You should really dig deep here. An important thing to look for is the sense that we desire something to make us feel "whole" or complete, a topic we'll cover in detail in Part IV.

2. *Evaluate your daily actions with these priorities in mind.* Do you prioritize all of these things as much as you'd like? Why not? Is there an unhealthy prioritization or an aspect of one of your priorities that is unwholesome that you should work on? Do you have too many things on your list? Be aware that you can only place your focus on so many things at once. The more on your plate so to speak, the less effective you'll be at managing each piece.

Once you've evaluated your daily actions and have seen whether or not they align with your priorities, it's your job to make the necessary adjustments for your life to match those priorities. If you want to place focus on your daily meditation practice, but you notice you spend way too much time on Facebook, even if it's in a wholesome way to connect with family and friends, then it may be smart to cut down on your use of Facebook if it's not as high of a priority to make space for your daily meditation.

Next comes simplifying your life. It's important to simplify your life in any possible way to reduce the potential for distractions and allow you the greatest ability to focus on your practice and priorities. That is a pretty large topic, so we'll go into detail on it in the next chapter. Lastly, after having simplified your life so that you can give your all to your practice and your priorities, it's simply the process of taking action with all of your being towards tending to your life in a wholesome way with those priorities as the focus. If your loved ones, daily mindful living practice, and work are your priorities then you'd be giving your all to them. This is something we've been working towards for some time now. Your mindful living practice, mindful consumption, one-pointed mind, and the work we'll do in the next chapter to simplify your life all stack together to create the right environment to give all of your being to these few focus efforts.

This Moment

Sounds simple enough from there, right? Unfortunately, though, that isn't the end of it. It's not always so easy to make a change. Once this has been done, and you begin acting based on your revised priorities, you'll notice something interesting. You don't necessarily follow through. It's always possible that you went through your priorities, maybe even changed nothing about them (your original unconscious priorities before doing this exercise), and perfectly followed through on them. However, the likelihood is, there are not only things which you should or would like to be prioritizing that you're not, but that even when establishing those things as priorities you'll find yourself having a hard time following through on them.

This last step is where your mindfulness practice and practice of living intentionally interweave. Be mindful of what arises in connection with your effort to follow through on these priorities. With time, you'll notice what is connected with these various efforts and be able to see clearly the culprit, leading to the opportunity to make a positive change. It's not always so simply, though, which is why we'll cover this in more detail in the last chapter of Part II, *Easeful Discipline and Establishing a Daily Practice*.

Simplifying Your Life

If I had to live with only a handful of things, what would they be?

Zen, the tradition I began my journey from and which I still practice today, is very concentrated and intentional. In living the life of a Zen monk, for instance, all fluff is removed and only the essentials remain. This is true for essentially all Buddhist monastics. This can truly help improve our life in meaningful ways, helping to remove that which is useless (or far less important) and potentially distracting and giving us more time for what matters most.

In *Mindful Consumption and the Garden of Consciousness*, we discussed mindful consumption and creating an environment more conducive to our practice of cultivating great peace and freedom. The effort of mindful consumption is very similar to the effort here of simplifying one's life, with some overlap, but the effort is distinctly different in a number of ways as well. It's important to have covered both mindful consumption and living with a single, or one-pointed, mind first because both are primary efforts. By that I mean simplifying your life should only come into the equation once both of those primary efforts have been acted on. Mindful consumption is about cutting your life down in the most meaningful way: discouraging the unwholesome seeds and encouraging the wholesome ones. What's left of that

This Moment

is what we work on further simplifying, with the primary effort being the reducing of potential distractions to your practice and priorities as a whole. And living with a one-pointed mind is about understanding clearly what's most important and living your life in a way that you promote that, exactly what simplifying your life is all about. But you can't, or at least it's unwise to, simplify your life until you know what's essential. In other words, what is important (a priority). Doing so is less than effective, if at all possible in the first place, to say the least.

By the time we're adults, we've generally amassed quite a lot of things in our lives which are either useless or relatively unimportant. Both material things and non-material things. The monastic way of life (for any spiritual tradition really) is designed so that only the essentials remain: physical nourishment, a place to rest, a community, and the practice.

Now, this might be a little extreme and even unnecessary to most, but the idea is what's most important. The idea is to remove everything in your life that isn't essential. Essential to what? Essential to your well-being, the well-being of others, and what's most important to you. But where do you begin? How do you decide what's essential and non-essential? The best place to start is to ask yourself if the item or thing is ever used or ever holds any purpose. If it's never used, or holds no purpose, those are the first and most obvious things to go.

From there it gets more difficult, but the questions to ask are simple:

Does this thing help contribute to the well-being of myself and those around me? Do I need this to be happy?

If the answer is no to either question then the likelihood is it not only doesn't serve a purpose but often gets in the way of allowing those things that really matter to shine in your life. Keep in mind that included within this is wholesome things which you simply enjoy doing, like reading articles online or playing a particular sport. It might not have a clear value as far as your mental well-being is concerned, but if it's something you truly enjoy doing then it is wholesome and very beneficial for you (provided it's a wholesome, or at least not harmful, activity). You can also go in the opposite direction by asking yourself:

If I had to live with only a handful of things, what would they be?

To me, this is the best starting point because this question immediately gets you to cut down to only what is essential. Again not just material possessions here but non-material things in activities, responsibilities, etc. This question can help distill your life down to it's essence. As an example, when I asked myself that question, I got this:

- *My family*
- *My practice*
- *Buddhaimonia / my work*
- *Laptop computer (strictly for Buddhaimonia / my work + study)*
- *Smartphone (strictly for family communication)*
- *My home*
- *Physical nourishment*
- *Basic set of clothes (few pairs of pants, shirts, one pair of shoes, socks, a jacket)*

You'll notice at this point that your answers to this exercise will start looking very similar to your priorities. This is to be expected due to the close alignment of simplifying your life and the effort we made in the last chapter to focus our life with a one-pointed mind. It might be beneficial to ask yourself that question a few times too, because sometimes you'll put down things you think are essential, but upon closer examination you realize they really aren't. That doesn't necessarily mean you'll want to give it up, but in any case it will give you clarity. From here, you can work backwards and look at your life. What exists in it now which wasn't included in this list? Why didn't you include it? Can you give it up? Should you? Would you have more time to focus on what's most important to you if you gave it up?

With the basic framework for simplifying your life outlined, let's now go over the major areas. In each point, I'll cover specific things I've done to simplify my own life which you can try out for yourself. These categories are:

1. *Finances*
2. *Email*
3. *Screen Time*
4. *Material Possessions*
5. *Actions*
6. *Social Distractions*
7. *Meal Time*
8. *Become a Conscious Consumer*

Finances

As I spoke about earlier in Living Intentionally, some topics within this part of the book might seem to veer off. But don't be mistaken, working to simplify your finances is a highly beneficial area of simplifying your life. The entire practice of simplifying your life is about reducing mental activity to cut back on distractions, resulting in less stress and anxiety and more space to breathe and focus on what's most important, and simplifying your finances allows you to do just that.

To begin working on this, first, put as many things on autopilot as possible. This means set your paycheck up on direct deposit (if it isn't already), set your bills up to automatically deduct from your account when they're due, and to align your bills so that they're all due on the same one or two days of the month. Also, set up a savings account and have it auto deduct every week when you get your deposit. If you can't afford to save much right now that's OK, just start by saving a few dollars a week. Whatever you can afford, what's most important is that you establish the habit now and begin working to create a small emergency fund, which can help save you from major headaches (which would otherwise be an additional source of stress and anxiety) in the future.

Second, reduce the number of accounts you have. Most importantly, take the shredder to your credit cards. They just waste your money, build bad spending habits, and are a source of additional stress. It's too easy to miss a payment and have your interest rate skyrocket to something crazy and then you're locked in debt and your credit score takes a hit. The one exception to this would be a prepaid credit card for the purpose of building your credit. If you're neck-high in credit card debt and that isn't an option, then you can consolidate your credit. This will take all of your credit card accounts and combine them into one easy to manage monthly payment. It will also take all of those annoying phone calls and letters off your back, which are a huge source of stress and anxiety.

Third, examine your monthly bills. Look to see if there's any services you don't actually use regularly. Maybe you haven't watched much TV in the past few months. It could be something small like a TV service such as Netflix or Hulu (with membership) or something larger like your cable bill. This will help simplify your monthly bills, which can be very nice.

Lastly, pay for weekly expenses with cash. By doing this you'll avoid the confusion of trying to look at your online banking and match up what you spent with your available balance. This is a headache. Each week take out the amount that you've pre-decided for your weekly expense category (groceries, gas, etc.) and separate them into stacks. You can hold them with money clips, in envelopes or any other way that works for you. This makes your weekly finances extremely clear and simple to work with. If you combine each of these points, there's the potential to drastically reduce the overall stress and anxiety caused by finances and limit its ability to distract you.

Email

If your email situation is anything like mine was, it can get out of hand without proper maintenance. About 95% of my emails go to one account now, but at one point, I had 5 or so email accounts and was checking my email some fifteen or more times per day. So, start by consolidating your email accounts. Closely examine exactly why you use each email account. By doing so you'll probably find that a few of those are either useless or can be merged into another account.

Next, unsubscribe from email lists you never use or gain any value from. This could be iTunes if you never gain any value from what is on the email list, Target if you don't shop at Target enough to care what's on their emails (or if you do and just don't care to see their emails either way like me) or some other company which you never had any particular interest in receiving emails from in the first place. I know for me there were quite a bit. This should help reduce the amount of emails you receive daily and leave the emails of greater importance.

Lastly, now that you've simplified your email accounts, set up a system. Most importantly establish a schedule where you only check your email once or twice a day. Commit to yourself that you won't open up your email outside of that block of time. This can really help to reduce daily distractions. The reality is, we don't need to check our email twenty times a day. If email is an important part of your day block out however much time you need and get to work. Focus on the high important emails first and get to however many others you can in the rest of that block of time. After that, move on. Don't let email rule your life and don't be scared of leaving emails unread.

Screen Time

This is a big one. Screens are a major force for distraction and mental dispersion in modern life. First, reduce your TV time or stop watching it altogether. If you only reduce your TV time, then at least watch online where there's little to no commercials (depending on the platform you use). This will save you time, reduce your commercial exposure and put you in better control of your time. You won't have to catch your favorite show exactly when it's on anymore, allowing you to be able to record it and watch it later. This greater flexibility and freedom leads to less stress and fewer potential distractions.

Next, reduce the amount of time you're on your smartphone. I'd suggest going through your smartphone and deleting any unused apps. When you have way too many possible distractions on your phone you tend to pick it up and look for things to distract yourself with. If you're on an iPhone, or another smartphone with similar functionality, you can bunch the remaining apps into folders to make them harder to get to and easier to forget about (but still having them there for when you actually need them). This is one of the more dangerous distractions in our everyday life because it's always there with us. By drastically reducing the amount of times you pick your phone up in a given day you'll notice you'll have a calmer and less dispersed mind.

I do thorough check-ups of my phone on a regular basis. The first time I did it I found that I rarely used or had no need for roughly 70% of the apps I had downloaded. I reduced the number of apps on my phone to one page and put any rarely used or undelete-able apps (iPhone...) into their own folder and threw them on the second page where I would never lay eyes on them. This drastically reduced the amount of time I wasted each day playing around on my phone doing nothing particularly important.

Material Possessions

Like most people, you probably have quite a few unnecessary material possessions which are taking up space and cluttering your life. Most of us don't notice the effect they have on us. However, when you take the time to clear away the material clutter in your life you'll find yourself with room to breathe that you never knew you had. It's pretty liberating to disconnect yourself from material possessions. Depending on whether or not you have kids (a big one), a significant other, a house (another big one), what you do for a living / enjoy doing on your off time and whether or not you're a pack rat you can have varied amounts of clutter. I have known some real pack rats in my life. Their emotional attachment to material items isn't healthy. It just keeps you from finding that true, renewable and limitless happiness that exists when you find out that happiness doesn't exist outside of you in material items. And the worst part is it's so difficult to notice when you suffer from it. But this isn't exclusive to pack rats. Actually, most of us have some form of unhealthy attachment to material items, albeit a subtler form.

So, how will you know what's clutter and what isn't? Use this benchmark:

1. *Do you ever use it? Does it provide any value? No? Probably need to trash it.*
2. *Do you use it but it wastes your time, creates additional distractions, and provides no positive*

value for you or anyone around you? Probably need to trash it.

3. *Do you use it and it provides positive value for you or others around you? Consider keeping it.*

After that gather everything up that's left and look at what's left. Cross-reference it with what's most important to you. Then, see if anything else comes to mind that's unnecessary. It might provide positive value but if you have fifty things like that and none of them are necessarily essential, it's still clutter that takes away from what's most important. What's left after this are the essentials.

Actions

We try to handle so many things at once. Both men and women are pressured in different ways from society at large. Both are expected to do so many things at once, do them all perfectly and all the while keeping face. We don't notice that this affects the way we act. However, we don't have to follow along with this agenda. In fact, keeping up with the Jones' only takes you further away from peace and freedom. In order to establish the life you want you need to be willing to be honest with yourself and those around you. When necessary, you need to be able to tell yourself, and those around you, *no*. This is an aspect of focusing on what's most important, what we spoke about in the last chapter. You'll still juggle from time to time, that's an aspect of modern life that's difficult to get around, but you can greatly reduce this. By simplifying your life at large it makes it that much easier to focus.

The bottom line is don't spread yourself thin, both in responsibilities and in commitments. If this is the case, you won't do a good job tending to any of your priorities. Focus on one or a few things at a time and give 100% of yourself to them.

Social Distractions

Everyone is on social media these days. You might visit Facebook once a day, check Twitter every couple of days or use multiple social accounts on a daily basis. Whatever your frequency or preference it's hard to escape the pull of digital socializing in the modern world. But, as great a resource as they can be for staying connected with friends, family, any of your other favorite people or things, they can become a major distraction. They can, and will, keep you from enjoying life without you even knowing it.

Making friends online is a lot easier to do then in person. And perhaps because of that there's an addicting quality to it. I know people who have at certain points made it a habit to check their Facebook, Twitter or Instagram accounts some 20, 30 or more times a day. For this reason, work on keeping your social time online to a minimum. This will greatly reduce daily distractions.

Being social online isn't bad, though. As I mentioned, it can be a very good thing. Just make sure you're careful about how much you're using it and what conversations you take part in. Don't follow people or take part in conversations just for the sake of gossiping or talking negatively about something or someone. That won't serve you and will just nourish unwholesome seeds in you.

Meal Time

When I say meal time I'm really talking about simplifying meal time by way of pre-planning your meals. Whether you're single or have a family, figuring out what you're going to eat (especially at dinner) can be a real headache. We live in an age where we're provided with so many different options that just deciding what to eat for dinner can be a task in itself (and sometimes a debate!).

Unless you're a robot I'm assuming you eat every single day, a few times a day. So, do yourself a favor: take some time to list out all the various dishes and foods you eat on a semi-regular basis. Separate this list based on meal time: breakfast, lunch, dinner and any other time you usually eat, if any. Also, take some time to list out high-energy snacks.

Second, sub-separate those categories into two sections based on the meals you cook/prepare and restaurants/fast food locations you visit.

Third, take this list and each week plan out your meals. This method helps reduce the amount of times you eat out each week and really simplifies the headache that mealtime can be. And you don't have to be so specific. You can buy milk & cereal and some berries and figure you'll have those on various days for breakfast without actually deciding which days specifically.

Lastly, go to the store that same day and buy all of the ingredients you'll need for the coming week. I know from experience that you'll sometimes forget things and still have to run by the store, but it will reduce the amount of times you need to do so in a given week (especially if you have kids). This method of pre-planning meals has greatly simplified the meal time process for me and my family. It reduces headache, cuts down on time, reduces grocery store runs and gives you that time back to focus on what's most important.

Become a Conscious Consumer

So, you've simplified your life in seven major areas. You're feeling pretty good. You have breathing room, less clutter, less distractions, less complications and life in general

This Moment

has just become more enjoyable. Overall, living more simply has become a great source of peace and happiness for you. But you need to maintain this in order for it to continue. You need to become a conscious consumer. Let your mindful awareness guide you here. When considering whether to consume or purchase something new, ask yourself: "Do I need this? Or can I live without it?" "Will this take time away from something else that's important to me? Am I OK with that?" and "Will this contribute to my life in a wholesome way?"

This includes all seven categories. Do so when you consider adding an account or a new bill to your financial situation, when you consider taking on a new goal or responsibility, when you consider trying out a new social network because a friend asks you to join her or when you consider buying something new for your home. In all of these scenarios ask yourself the questions I listed above.

I can't tell you what the right choice is to make, only you can do that. However, as long as you stay mindful and make a more aware decision based on your life you can maintain a simpler and more peaceful lifestyle, one which promotes and supports your practice of mindful, meditative and intentional living and what is most important to you.

Easeful Discipline and Establishing a Daily Practice

It's the existence of order in this way that allows for our practice, and our lives, to blossom.

Now that we've essentially covered everything with regards to establishing the proper environment for a nourishing life and effective practice, what's left? All that's left is the specific effort you make in each moment. By that I mean the *quality* of your effort. So far, we've covered in detail the first two of the three steps I mentioned in One-Pointed Mind. Here's a refresher:

With regards to living with a one-pointed mind, this involves:

1. Deciding what's beneficial and most important to you.
2. Simplifying your life (cutting down on the nonessentials/distractions).
3. And giving yourself fully to those beneficial and important things.

This Moment

In *One-Pointed Mind*, we discussed not only the overarching effort with regards to honing in on what is most important and how to live in a way that we promote that, but we went into the detail on how to decide what is most beneficial and important to you (point #1). Then, in the last chapter, we covered point #2- simplifying your life- in great detail. In this chapter, the final chapter of Part II: *Living Intentionally*, we'll cover point #3, giving yourself fully to what's most important.

So, back to the point at hand. What is the right type of effort? What are its defining characteristics, things you can take with you and apply directly and clearly to your daily life? Those are the questions this chapter seeks to answer in clear and concise terms. With regards to that, there are three major points to cover. These are the three defining characteristics of the right quality effort to promote your practice and encourage wholesome action:

1. *Living and practicing with discipline.*
2. *Living and practicing with a sense of easefulness and joy.*
3. *Living and practicing with knowledge of one's habitual tendencies.*

Ultimately, this chapter is about the quality of your effort and how that affects our ability to live fully and freely as well as how the quality of that effort communicates into daily practice. Also, keep in mind, mindfulness itself could be considered a defining characteristic of the right effort to make in each moment. A mindful effort is, of course, very important as we've already spoken about. However, I'm talking more about how you approach your mindfulness and meditative practice itself than anything else, and we've already covered mindfulness in detail, so it's not included here.

Establishing Order

In a very real way, it's order which gives us true freedom. Many of us are afraid of order, of structure, but this is generally due to a misunderstanding. Order is the foundation of discipline, the first of the three defining characteristics.

Think about it this way: what if you could free up an entire hour each day for yourself if you just took the time to establish a daily schedule and stuck to it with discipline? What if this was a real possibility? Isn't this more time freedom? Also, it's by setting up this sense of order that we can occasionally break away, and this can be very liberating. Without a sense of order, we not only wander aimlessly and waste our precious time, but can can't create the right environment for freedom to arise.

To live half-asleep, unconscious to so much of what we do (even though our bodies are doing it), is the opposite of true freedom. Living in this way, we're being pushed and pulled by our habitual patterns and being directed by the winds of life. To live our lives in a way that we structure our days and live with a sense of order is to live with freedom because we're living intentionally. To live intentionally is to live mindfully, knowing that you're placing one foot forward. If you live like this, you're taking that step. To take that step mindfully, to know you're taking that step and to do it with mindful awareness, is true freedom. And it is order, and the discipline which grows from that sense of order, which helps us live in this way.

With this sense of order established, which in everyday application really just involves having a schedule, sticking to it diligently, and setting important rules for when life gets in the way of scheduled tasks, such as our meditation practice, discipline is possible. Without it, sticking to anything can be very difficult. Keep in mind, this doesn't have to be anything severe, simply a general sense of order and structure which allows for your practice of cultivating greater peace and freedom to unfold in a reliable way. Remember, it's the existence of order in this way that allows for our practice, and our lives, to blossom.

Sometimes, we think that things like "order" and "structure" are boring and useless (or, at best, mildly useful), when in fact when used in the right way they can be the breeding ground for much peace, joy, and freedom. A daily routine, for instance, allows for a quieter mind because there's less to think about. Ultimately, that's really what you want- less to think about = more enjoying the peace of the present moment and the development of your practice. In modern life, planning ahead and remembering certain things is necessary to a point, but by structuring things in the right way and pre-planning, we can remove much of that mental clutter that builds up as a result of our many everyday tasks, to-do's, and important events. And sure, life gets in the way sometimes no matter what we do, but in my experience this is still highly effective despite that.

We're so afraid of forgetting what we have to do that we often feel the need to cycle thoughts repeatedly through our mind until the time comes to do them. The thing is, that cycle never ends because new things come up. So our minds are constantly cluttered with, "Remember this!", and "Remember that!" By establishing a daily routine and some form of order to your life, you remove a lot of feeling that you need to do that. And, as a result, you remove more mental clutter and give yourself more peace and freedom.

So, what should this daily routine we just spoke about actually look like? That's completely up to your own life as a whole. To some degree, that will change day-by-day, but as long as you make your major daily (or weekly) activities routine to some degree than you'll have done a great deal. Outside of that, I'd suggest keeping a simple to-do list of the three to four most important things you have to do that day.

Don't let this to-do list rule your life though, only use it to keep a few important points for that day (or group of days). I've found this to not only be the most effective type of to-do list productivity wise, but it's simplicity keeps it from becoming its own monster (to-do lists are helpful, but only to a point). I prefer Trello (trello.com) due to its simplicity, but you could use anything.

Having some form of structure keeps you from wasting time. It improves your efficiency towards the task at hand because you act with more of your being in every moment. On top of that, breaking that sense of order and structure from time to time can become a very liberating experience. Zen monasteries have always been run with a sense of order and structure because they're perfectly aware of the power of it. Zen priests didn't run monasteries with a strong sense of order just because they felt like it- everything in Zen is calculated- they did it to create a breeding ground for those students to better realize insight and their true nature. Use a sense of order and structure to liberate yourself in your own life by creating a daily routine, giving yourself more mental energy for what really matters.

Easeful and Joy-Filled Practice

The second principle is to live and practice in an easeful and joy-filled way. This is possibly the most important point in this chapter, because it's something most people are lacking. The way most of us live we have some semblance of discipline, but altogether lack an understanding of the importance to live and practice with a sense of easefulness and joy, pushing ourselves as hard as we will go and resulting in a lot of additional stress, anxiety, and overall suffering.

To walk the mindful path, to live intentionally, and to make meditation a part of your daily life is a pursuit which should be taken seriously, even if for no other reason than the fact that it helps us greatly in our efforts to live more fully and freely in each moment of our life. However, discipline without a sense of joy and easefulness is harmful and ineffective. Sure, maybe you can become an accomplished businessman with nothing more than discipline, creativity, and resourcefulness, but if you don't live and work in an easeful and joy-filled way, then it'll all be for nothing because you'll end up at "success" with stress, anxiety, and potentially even depression born from intense paranoia and loneliness (something common in cntrepreneurs). If that's the case, then what is the point? Remember, as we spoke about in the beginning of the book, this type of effort is misguided. It's ultimately a misunderstanding of what matters most. However, to live and practice in a way that you understand this basic principle, that what we all want is simply peace and freedom for ourselves and others, you immediately see the value in doing so not just with discipline but also with a sense of ease and joy.

What does this look like in daily life? Giving yourself enough time to move from place to place (as we spoke about in Part I, *Making Mindfulness a Way of Life*), taking regular breaks in between strenuous work (which has shown to be more productive, mind you- see the *Pomodoro Technique*) to breathe or walk mindfully, or taking the time to appreciate what's around you as you go about your day: a flower, a tree, animals, the water, people coming together, the smile of a child, the smile on someone's face after you've helped open a door or pick up their things for them, the joy of music, the blue sky, and anything else you can think of. When we live mindfully, deeply touching our life in every moment, we learn to appreciate what once seemed insignificant. In this way, we can touch joy and cultivate a sense of easefulness in everything we do. This is what it means to move throughout your life both with a sense of discipline towards your practice and a sense of easefulness and joy.

Of course, this is sometimes easier said than done. But remember that this section is titled *Living Intentionally*. It's your *intention* to make your best effort in each moment as well as to accept whatever comes to be after that.

Establishing a Daily Practice with Minimal Resistance

The last point, #3, is about living and practicing with awareness of our habitual tendencies. To practice or make an effort of any kind without a firm grasp of this, and without having taken action to combat it, is to leave yourself unguarded against a powerful force. There are many ways harmful habitual patterns can manifest, but with regards to daily mindfulness and meditation practice there is one principle I want to focus in on. That's the tendency for us to lean towards what we feel is easiest in any given moment, or as I tend to call it, *the path of least resistance.*

The path of least resistance is something I talk about often- and for good reason. It tells the story of our natural tendency to prioritize whatever is easiest to do in a given moment. For this reason, it's both a great enemy of establishing new positive habits as well as a powerful force which can be utilized if you learn the basic idea behind it. There are two basic sides to the equation of utilizing the path of least resistance:

1. *Discouraging what you consider to be unwholesome habits.*
2. *Encouraging what you consider to be wholesome habits.*

For instance, if you want to begin eating more mindfully, but you're so used to eating mindlessly, scarfing down your food, you can:

This Moment

1. *Start chewing each bite 30 times.*
2. *If you eat with a fork, turning it so that it points upside down. Or, if possible, eating with chop sticks.*
3. *Sometimes eat your food when it's either very hot or very cold. Or...*
4. *Sometimes eat food that takes work to consume, like nuts or shellfish.*
5. *Switch hands. Right-handed? Eat with your left. Or, better yet, switch hands with chop sticks.*
6. *Regularly eat your meal in a totally different room (or outside).*
7. *Designate a mindful snack. Have one specific food that you dedicate yourself to eat mindfully. Oftentimes focusing in on one activity to do mindfully and not worrying about the rest helps quite a bit.*

Each one of these points will make a small difference, but if you pair a few of these together, you'll have a pretty effective strategy for eating more mindfully. You'll notice that the general idea here is that you're making it *more* difficult to eat mindlessly and *encouraging* mindful eating. That's the essence of utilizing the path of least resistance.

This doesn't just work for mindful eating, though. This principle can be applied to anything and everything to help encourage and support your daily practice and general effort of living more fully and freely in the present moment. This can be applied to encourage your daily sitting meditation practice, to help encourage you to be mindful each morning when you wake up and to continue to be throughout your day, or to do an individual practice (like we talked about with mindful eating) more consistently.

Know that your habitual patterns won't ever give you a break. Your past conditioning will constantly push and pull at you to do something other than what you want to do. Your mindfulness practice is a valuable ally in identifying and then rewriting these habitual patterns, but you'll need more than just mindfulness practice to create a strong and consistent daily practice. That's where the path of least resistance comes in.

Make Your Best Effort

It's important to remember that you're making your best effort. That's what we're always doing (or, at least, trying to do). We're always just making our way as best as we can in this life. That's all we can do. Remember that it's important for your effort to be joyful and pleasant. If your practice itself seems strenuous and a cause of stress in itself, that's not the right effort.

Moving forward, beyond what we've spoken about so far with regards to establishing a daily practice, what if you're not practicing the right effort? What if you're not sticking with your practice? Still following bad old habits? What else is left that can be done? This often means you haven't found a way of practice which works for you or you don't yet see the benefit. You need to try out different ways of practicing, forms, methods, times, people, locations, etc. and find what feels best to you. Also, take time to remind yourself why you were originally attracted to the practice in the first place (remember: *Reaffirm Your Practice*).

It's inevitable that you'll fall off of your practice from time-to-time. This happens to everyone. The best you can do is to just reevaluate your situation and find out where the holes, or leaks, are. Patch things up and move forward. And sometimes, there are no holes and you just need to get back on track. We make the greatest progress when we lean in to our challenges, so make it a point to welcome stumbles, learn from them and grow.

This Moment

Part III: Living Naturally

This Moment

Opening Yourself Fully to This Moment

"The pain that you create now is always some form of nonacceptance, some form of unconscious resistance to what is."

- Eckhart Tolle

I have to open up about something. Up until this time, you may have had the wrong idea about what this practice we've been exploring really looks like in everyday life. Sure, some days it will pan out exactly as you planned it, but a lot of times that's not the case. And I don't just mean simply distractions and responsibilities getting in the way of your practice like we spoke about in Part II, I mean big things holding you back from your greater effort of living fully and freely in the present moment. That's the purpose of Part III: *Living Naturally.*

Living Naturally is about overcoming challenges-seeing through wrong perceptions, learning how to more skillfully navigate life's challenges, and getting out of your own way. But more specifically, it's about living in harmony with the world around you, with the "ultimate/basic truths" of this life. This why I titled it *Living Naturally*, because to live naturally is to live in harmony with these great truths: the truth of impermanence, interbeing, of resistance, and expressing our true nature. Learning how to live naturally, in harmony with the world around you, is ultimately about learning how to live more skillfully more than any other section in the book (although the entire book is about that, really).

This first chapter is about a basic principle which affects our entire lives. A truth most of us never realize, and as a result, we suffer endlessly always trying to fix the problem in a way that just makes it worse. It's *resistance*. In many ways, this is the foundational principle which every other chapter in this part shows a different perspective of.

This principle has been described many ways before, but I prefer resistance because it gives you what I feel is an accurate visual representation of what the real thing happening is in each moment. We're resisting what is, to put it simply. There's really nothing more to it. This is the basic reason why we suffer in every way. We're fighting against the natural way of things instead of working to live in harmony. But why are we resisting, especially when that resistance is causing friction in our lives, which leads us to suffering?

Resisting This Moment

All our lives, we were taught that there's "bad" and "good" and that these are very separate things, one which we should avoid and one which we should try to get more of. But this is very misleading. This is because, without the bad, there would be no good. You wouldn't have the capability to identify happiness if it weren't for your challenges and struggles. These challenges and struggles should be appreciated, because they allow the opportunity for us to experience the beauty and joy that life has to offer.

If we can begin to remove this dualistic thinking and see that without the bad, without the challenges, there would be no good, no beauty or peace or joy, we can begin to transform our relationship with those occurrences so that they no longer affect us the way that they once did. And, going a bit deeper, much of what we identify as "bad", "annoying", etc. is only so because of the concept we hold in our minds.

Much of the suffering we feel exists because of:

Something happens -> Touches mind, Idea (or combination of ideas) triggered -> Creates suffering

It's when the event registers in our minds that we draw a judgment on it that leads us to resist it. This is, again, something we've been taught since we were little ("This is bad." "That's good."). This takes non-dualistic thinking to another level: preventative. This is all about living in a way that we simply don't draw judgment and accept what we're faced with fully as it comes.

In this way, those things you once considered "bad" no longer affect you the same as they once did, and you can even oftentimes find joy in them. This principle of resistance is closely connected to living without expectations, understanding that it's not the traffic which caused us to become angry, it was the expectation in our minds that we would have a swift drive home which triggered the anger when we encountered the traffic. It is these expectations which are a big part of our resistance in everyday life. Of course, that's hardly enough explanation to know how to actually apply this in your own life. To better understand this and see clearly how you can apply it, I'll give some personal examples.

Before my first son was born I experienced paralyzing anxiety due to my money troubles. Any time I'd think about money I'd go into a sort of shock and freeze up completely. This wasn't just stressful and a source of anxiety, it was the most unproductive thing I could possibly do to actually get out of my situation in the first place. It took some time, but after a while, I was able to step away from the issue and separate myself from it due to the clarity I had found through my mindfulness practice. At times, I still experienced challenges due to a lack of money, but it no longer affected me the way that it once did.

Ultimately, this was partly because my mindfulness practice allowed me to face the issue, but I still needed to open up and have the courage to face it. My practice forced me to face up to it and observe it more closely and at length. And, after a while, that paralyzing and anxiety-causing quality to it dropped away as I gained greater clarity.

There are many ways this can manifest in the garden of our consciousness, which as you'll recall holds many seeds- seeds of anger, resentment, fear, jealousy, and more. However, it all comes down to the same one thing- resistance to the present moment. It will take time before you can spot this resistance yourself, but over time, you'll be able to see it more clearly and with dedication to your practice you'll begin to let go of it and live with greater peace and freedom.

Another clear example from my own life is when I found out I was going to be a father...for the third time. I initially resisted the idea of being a father for the third time and found myself feeling resentment and anger towards the unborn child. Don't worry though, it has a happy ending. Here is that story:

The Freak Out

"If a man has nothing to eat, fasting is the most intelligent thing he can do."

- Herman Hesse

This Moment

Two weeks ago, I found out I was going to be a father. For the third time. We didn't plan it. I'll get back to that in a sec.

The way we normally go about our lives, our brains use our "local" consciousness to gather information and make both small and larger predictions in order to create the best chance for our survival. And generally, as humans, we're often not just trying to survive, but we're trying to take steps to thrive. Specifically, to overcome our troubles and find peace, to be happy and enjoy our lives, and to forge some sense of greater meaning.

But because we only have so much power to change the world around us, and because our predictions can't be right 100% of the time, we're constantly hit with surprises- events which we didn't predict or expect would arise (i.e. the curveball). So we do our best to not only predict what will happen so as to be ready for it, but also to affect the world around us in our favor in various ways. But what do we do when shit totally hits the fan (as it does, so often)?

When I found out I was going to be a father for the third time, on the cusp of my wife and I's upcoming wedding (we never had a formal ceremony), writing and working like a madman on everything Buddhaimonia (so many awesome things in the works!), and the already full-time job that is taking care of our two little dudes, I was honestly a little freaked out and questioned whether we'd be able to handle it. What on Earth were we going to do? She already had a hard enough time taking care of these two crazy dudes during the day while I worked, what were we going to do with a third?

On top of that, the community at Buddhaimonia has really taken off, was this going to crush that? Was I just going to be so busy taking care of my 3 children that this amazing project I've devoted so much of my life to was just going to rot from neglect? I started to flashback to all the conversations I've had with so many of you through the past couple of months, all the great things that are happening here and will happen in the future, and the force for good Buddhaimonia could grow into in the future. Then I instinctively imagined my books, notes, and all of Buddhaimonia burning in a great big fire, never to be seen again.

It's all over man, why did you have to do it?

Shining a Light

...All of that went through my mind over the course of about 2 minutes. Our minds can do the most irrational things at times. Once I came to, grounding myself with my mindful breathing, I did a few things:

1. I recognized the emotions running through me with my mindfulness and simply observed them for a while, seeing that they weren't attached to rational thought or were in any way sensible.
2. I realized the amazing gift that this new child would be and accepted her or him fully in my mind with love (don't go through a pregnancy despising your future child for what they kept you from doing, it's a sure way to depression and resentment).
3. I thought more closely about the fact that our oldest son Malik could actually be a big help to my wife and I with regards to taking care of this new baby.
4. I reminded myself of my growing flexibility with my work and I reaffirmed that nothing would ever keep me from giving my best effort to this, Buddhaimonia, which I've put my heart and soul into.

But most of all, I openly and consciously accepted everything as it was, including whatever may come. Now, I couldn't feel better about the whole situation. I know it won't be easy, but what ever is? I chose the Herman Hesse quote above because it perfectly describes my point:

Accept everything openly and mindfully as it is. Resistance creates friction which keeps you from peace.

Life is not a straight path. If it were, we could see clearly each next step and be able to prepare for it. That's just not how life is- no matter how hard you try to make it that way. Not having food to eat might sound like an extreme example, but it gets the point across perfectly. If you don't have food to eat, and you're constantly thinking and stressing about the fact that you don't have food to eat, that's pressure you're placing on yourself. But accept the fact that you don't have food, and decide in your mind that you're fasting, and as a result of accepting the situation as it is you'll release the friction keeping you from being at peace.

Resisting the natural flow of life is like purposely pressing your hand up against a sanding belt. It's definitely not going to feel very good and as much as you try to stop the sanding belt with your hand you're just going to end up hurting yourself more. This is how most of us live our lives. We don't even notice that it's our resistance which is causing the friction, the suffering in our lives, and not the event itself. Some of this is easier said than done, admittedly, but no less true. What's important isn't perfection, it's simply that you make your best effort in each moment. That will be enough. You've got your entire life to work at it.

The Monk and the Geisha

I figured it'd be wise to explain this idea in a little more detail as this is a topic easily misunderstood. There's an old Zen story about a priest and a geisha that perfectly exemplifies this point:

This Moment

A Zen Buddhist priest was among a group of guests who were attending a dinner party one evening. In traditional Japanese style, the guests were all seated on the floor surrounding a low rectangular table.

Resting on the table in front of each guest was a small hibachi grill filled with hot coals. Each guest cooked their own portion of meat and vegetables, which were brought out by geisha's and placed in various areas of the table.

The priest noticed that one of the geisha's conducted herself as if she might have had some Zen training. He decided to test her, so he called her over. The geisha knelt across the table from the priest and bowed. The priest bowed in return and said, "I would like to give you a gift." Using his chopsticks, he reached into the hibachi, picked up a hot coal, and offered it to the geisha. She hesitated for a moment, then finally pulled the sleeves of her kimono down over her hands. She grabbed the coal, ran into the kitchen, and dropped it into a pan of water. Her hands were not hurt, but the beautiful kimono gown was ruined.

When the geisha returned with a new kimono, she went back to the table and knelt across from the priest. She bowed to the priest. He bowed in return. Then she said: "I would like to give you a gift as well." "I would be honored" the priest replied. She picked up a pair of chopsticks, removed a hot coal from the priest's grill, and offered it to him. The priest reached into his robe and took out a cigarette. As he leaned forward to light his smoke he said,

"Thank you. That is exactly what I wanted."

In this story, the priest, as well as the geisha, exemplify the true spirit of Zen. In the case of the geisha, she could have easily gotten angry at the priest. But the only thing anger would have done would be to burn her. Instead, she accepted the piece of coal with her unrolled kimono and went into the other room to dispose of it and change. In the case of the priest, he didn't just, "roll with it" so to speak, he adapted the coal as a light for his cigarette. Both the priest and the geisha adapted to their situations and accepted what was presented to them without creating friction.

This may just be a story, but one which highlights an important point: to go with the natural flow of things is part of the path to peace and harmony within oneself. Keep in mind, this doesn't mean you should lie down and take whatever comes at you and live without goals or intentions. There is a time to act, but it should be done in the spirit of naturalness instead of in the spirit of resisting what is. It should also be done while considering the well-being of others as well as ourselves. And we should live mindfully in order to observe when we're creating that friction in order to be able to identify what's the natural way in the first place.

When to Push, When to Go with It

Right about now, if you've been following along closely, you might be confused as to just how you're supposed to know when to push and when to go with the flow and adapt. There's no science to it, it's mostly intuitive. For the most part, it's our "broad" or greater intentions which make up the majority of our "pushing" efforts. For instance: deciding you're going to build a business, save for a house, or work towards a promotion. And it's life in the moment which is where we must adapt and "go with the flow". We set goals or intentions and life moves along naturally, without any mind for those goals or intentions. In this way, life can often seem as though it's trying to keep us from accomplishing our goals, but it's really just impartial.

So when we set goals or intentions, and something gets in the way, the best thing to do isn't to give up on that goal or to fight back and continue to try to make it happen as is, but to adapt and accomplish it by going with the natural flow of things. In general, friction is caused because we fight back against what's presented to us. But we fight back because we had other plans or desires in the first place, something else we wanted to happen in a certain situation. So it's those plans and predictions which are causing us to want to fight back against reality.

So don't hesitate to set goals or make big plans, simply do so without any attachment to them or to the way you originally expected to do or accomplish said thing. If something changes, you accept those changes openly and move with them.

Have Courage

The ability to adapt at a moment's notice to the curveballs of life, whether big or small, while not labelling them bad and just going with the natural flow of life is a big deciding factor in our ability to maintain our peace of mind. By doing so, you consciously decide that you don't derive your peace and happiness from external events but rather the deeper and ever-flowing "thusness" of life (resting in the present moment, feeling the interconnectedness of all of life) which is always available to us no matter what's going on in our lives. If you're constantly reacting negatively to change, whether big or small, whether it's trying to push or pull to change reality into something you believe more pleasant or

This Moment

just getting bitter and angry over what's already happened, then you'll be frequently unhappy with your life.

In the "modern" world, there's such a strong sense of, "Fight back!" "Resist!" "Make/Change your destiny!" And to do so while not only ignoring our own well-being but the well-being of others. There's nothing wrong with living purposely, but if you live your life thinking you're always fighting back against it and everything in it then you're just placing your hand on that sanding belt again.

I grew up in the U.S., so I can't speak for anywhere else, but most Americans have a strong sense of this. Most of us grew up thinking that life was a constant pushing and pulling, fighting against the odds, against the "forces", and making it happen no matter what. And while this mentality can help accomplish tasks, it creates a lot of harm too.

Going with the natural flow of things isn't a sign of weakness, it's a sign of strength and courage. It takes both to accept that you're not completely in control and to realize that you don't need to be. By doing so, you'll be well on your way to finding peace.

Being Yourself in Every Moment

Being yourself is acting in a way that nothing keeps you from expressing your true nature.

What does it mean to be yourself? What does it mean to express yourself honestly? To be authentic? A lot of people throw around words like that, but what do they really mean? And how do we actually do it? Surely, there's more to it than just choosing your clothes, hair color, and profession? I think most people really have no idea what it means to be yourself and simply say it out of a mild intuition that this is the right thing to do.

I don't want to throw out phrases and just say things without being very clear about what I mean. We shouldn't get hung up on language, but when we do use it we should closely analyze the words which we use, their intended meaning, and how we're using them in that specific moment. Here's a running definition so we have something to work with:

Being yourself is acting in a way that nothing keeps you from expressing your true nature.

This Moment

For many of us, they are the hardest things we will ever do: to face the fear of what others think of us, to work through the inner dialogue that keeps us questioning our self-worth and perpetuating the feeling of voidness (*something* is missing) and to push further to the deepest reaches of spiritual practice to reunite with, and fully express, our true nature. In this chapter, we'll shed light on each of these challenges, talk about the common thread that ties them all together, and cover the key practices to begin working through them.

"*I want blue hair*, but my co-workers will think I'm a childish fool who needs to get a life." You may or may not want blue hair, but we've all played out some version of that scene in our minds at one point or another, whether you realize it or not. This is the surface level of expressing yourself truly, honestly, naturally. This can include such things as your physical appearance, who you associate with, what profession you choose or how you choose to spend your time, among other things. In general, this includes more clearly overarching life choices and decisions as opposed to the next two levels.

Beyond that, there is the internal dialogue, which holds us back from taking action, as well as expressing your true nature, which is really what all of Part III: *Living Naturally*, is about. The internal dialogue is something we discussed in Part I, *Making Friends with Yourself*, via the story of my old Toms shoes. The internal dialogue is an old record of sorts, a collection of phrases that cycle through our mind on a regular basis. They bring us down and hold us back in countless ways, all essentially centering around the idea, "you're not good enough". In this way, the internal dialogue indirectly deals with the topic and is about much more than expressing yourself truly and naturally, but it is still a huge factor to keep in mind with regards to this. This level is a bridge between the more overarching life decisions of the first level and the more moment-to-moment practice of expressing your true nature, the next level.

Expressing your true nature is the "point" of Zen practice as to fully express one's true nature is to realize true peace and freedom, so this phrase is thrown around a lot in Zen circles. To live naturally, to express your true nature, is to live in harmony with all there is and exactly what this part of the book attempts to help you do. To live naturally is the highest calling on the path to being yourself. Your true nature *is* your true "self". This is much more moment-to-moment self-expression than the surface level of expressing yourself honestly. In each moment, are you acting in a way that conditioning- such as the fear of impermanence or attachment to an idea- is holding you back from expressing yourself truly and naturally? These are the things to watch for in the practice of expressing your true nature. But are these things in conflict with one another? Specifically, is the "surface level" of expressing ourselves honestly in the face of assumptive (or probable) criticism just an illusion? Should we not worry about physical expression, preferences, doing the things we enjoy, or expressing ourselves creatively? Are these things worthless? Not at all, each place on the path to expressing yourself naturally is worthwhile.

In Part I, *Making Friends with Yourself*, I told the story of a hospice nurse who interviewed her patients to discover their greatest regrets:

One of the first projects I worked on when starting Buddhaimonia was a series on the top regrets of the dying. There was a story floating around the internet at the time about a woman by the name of Bronnie Ware and a book she wrote about her time working as a hospice nurse. During her time, she essentially interviewed her patients and asked them what they're biggest regrets were. Surprisingly, they all said about the same five or so things. But I wanted to take it further, so I took those regrets and looked for the recurring themes, to find out what they essentially all boiled down to. Do you know what was essentially the one major regret? It was:

Living in a way that the person cared (or cared too much) what other people thought of them and their actions.

Caring what others think of us is a paralyzing fear, one of the greatest fears of all to be sure. This single fear can dictate nearly everything we do in every moment. It can dictate what we wear, where we go each day, what we say, what and who we listen to, what we watch, what we do on a small scale (whether or not we smoke that cigarette our friend offers us in high school) to what we do on a large scale (whether we pursue our passion to be a painter, as opposed to becoming a lawyer or a doctor like our parents want). It's so far-reaching that it gets to a point where it becomes extremely difficult to detect. Most of us right now go about our daily lives caring quite a bit about what others think of us and letting that negatively affect (at least, to some degree) what we do and how we do it.

However, to live your entire life in this way is to live a life of regret, as we can see so clearly illustrated by Bronnie Ware's personal experience. It means to go through your entire life doing things through the filter of what we think others might think of us only to end up on our deathbed regretting them and having no way to get that precious time back. So, clearly, expressing yourself fully and honestly is an important effort, one which deserves our full attention.

Major Factors

So, we have a much better idea of what it means to be ourselves and to express our true nature, but how do you actually go about expressing yourself more truly and naturally? First, let's get clear on the two major factors which keep us from walking the path to expressing ourselves more honestly and naturally so that we have clarity to work towards a resolution:

Major Factor 1: Fearing what others will think and/or do

This is the surface level we've spoken about thus far, so there isn't much to say here. Keep in mind that included within this major factor is the internal dialogue, which plays a huge role in perpetuating these fears.

Major factor 2: Conditioning

This can also include the internal dialogue, as our life experience may have conditioned us to break ourselves down and degrade ourselves, but this is most notably the deeper level of expressing your true nature. At this level, there is also a lot of fear present, but they're in deeper issues such as the fear of death and the impermanence of all things (which we'll talk about in the next chapter). When I say conditioning, I mean that there are certain factors which have built up (or were constructed) within us that affect the way we think, feel, and act. This can range from a specific type of fear, to a misunderstanding, to acting in a certain way when something very specific occurs within your life. Conditioning is something we're all affected by in almost every moment of our lives. And the difficult part is we don't notice it at all. In many ways, this is what the meditative path and the realizing of insight is about: to see clearly beyond the clouds that have formed over these conditions so that we can undo this conditioning and live freely. Other examples are dualistic "good" vs. "bad" thinking and the deepest level of all: the Buddha's Five Aggregates, which make up our sense of a separate self.

Working to realize and express your true nature, because it plays a big part in the path to peace and freedom, is the primary focus here. However, it doesn't mean that the surface level of working to express yourself honestly is useless, working through this fear that dominates over our lives is also very important and can be very liberating in itself (remember *the shoes*?). And also, by the way, it's not a set of steps, one-two-three. You don't have to overcome this fear of what others think of you before really getting serious about your meditation practice and working through these more major issues we discuss in this part of the book. These things happen at the same time. Some people think that if you meditate you're never supposed to get angry or be fearful or something, but that's not how it is. You can better manage fear and anger and the various challenges you encounter, but you're working through them gradually. It's not an overnight thing. It takes a lot of work, a lot of time and effort. We all start out with both conditioning and deep-seated issues in the way of fearing what others think of us and an internal dialogue that will take years to work through. This is perfectly normal.

How to Express Yourself More Naturally

Now that we have some clarity on the two major factors holding us back, let's talk about how to begin working through these factors to express ourselves more naturally (which I'll use from here on to refer to both expressing ourselves honestly and expressing our true nature). I gave some distinct examples in the first chapter of Part III, plus, we covered the internal dialogue in detail in Part I: *How to Make Friends with Yourself*, so you already have quite a bit to work with.

It's important to mention once again how important the practice of mindfulness is here. Mindfulness and meditation helps us not only uncover the internal dialogue that criticizes us, it also helps us notice the ways in which we resist moment-to-moment, such as in our expectations of how the world around us is going to (or supposed to) operate and how we push, pull, and attach to thoughts and ideas, all of which keeps us from expressing ourselves naturally (which we'll cover in detail in the last chapter of Part III).

Also, to begin expressing yourself more naturally, it can be very beneficial to "hone in" on fear as it arises, eventually with greater clarity identifying where it comes from, and working to mindfully and lovingly accept and embrace it, allowing it to be just as it is. This can create a great amount of healing and allow you to eventually work through the issue entirely, all depending on what it is. However, there's more to it than that.

These issues of self-worth, as well as the conditioning which has developed within the mind, only arise because of an attachment to the self- the "I"- the sense of a separate and unconnected self. By that I don't mean we aren't a separate body and brain or that our physical body somehow doesn't exist. Rather, this is the understanding that our fundamental nature is of this seemingly separate being which in fact interacts and intersects with other entities (people, things) in countless and ever-present ways in each and every moment. In other words, to say that we're this separate entity, at any point in our lives, is a considerable misunderstanding.

In old Zen monasteries, masters would place students in a position where their ego, the fortress of "I", was gradually eroded, eventually realizing freedom from everything in connection with this false sense of an ego, the ultimate cause of all suffering. This separate sense of a self is a big topic, one which is better put into practice than placed into words, so begin challenging your ego at every little opportunity and hold no presumptions about yourself, the world, or the way you live. It's in challenging and inspecting your daily experiences that you can come to gain true clarity and loosen the hold of the ego. Remember what I spoke about with regards to challenging the ego in Part I: *Making Friends with Yourself*:

1. *Accept that you have to get uncomfortable*
2. *Have courage*
3. *Be mindful*
4. *...and be kind & compassionate with yourself*

Oddly enough, it's in expressing yourself more truly in an outward surface way that you can begin to challenge the ego and work on a much deeper level, consequently working on both levels (because, as you can see now, from level one down to level three, it's all a matter of the ego). Now, I'm not necessarily telling you to dye your hair blue (unless you want to), but I am saying think of something you've put off, either recently or for a long time. You might have to sit down for a bit and really think hard about this. Once you have it, make it a resolution to finally do it, whatever it is. If some time has gone by since you originally put off doing said thing, make sure there's still going to be some mental push-back there (people you know who you think might criticize you, etc.), otherwise the exercise won't work. It's little persistent efforts such as this which can quickly begin to show you some semblance of freedom. And it's in shaving away at this sense of a separate self that we ultimately learn how to be ourselves, our true self, in every moment.

Living as If You're Going to Die in This Moment

"Throughout this life, you can never be certain of living long enough to take another breath."

- Zen master Huang Po

To live as if you're going to die is to live in a way that you're aware of your own impermanence and the impermanence of all things. Most of us live in a way that we ignore and even push away any thought of our own end, as well as the end of our loved ones, going to great lengths to either bottle it down or avoid it. However, this is a great mistake, because to live more aware of our own impermanence can be a great source of joy. By living in this way, we appreciate life so much more and are constantly reminded of the precious nature of this life that we're living. Each moment that you're reminded of your own impermanence is a moment in which flowers seem more vibrant, the fragrance of trees seems to grow stronger, and the cold air crisper.

It can be difficult to face the fact of our own impermanence, and often much more difficult to face the fact of the impermanence of every one and every thing around us. However, it's a fact which we must learn to face if we ever hope to live our life fully without regret. By pushing through those difficult feelings we can in fact realize a deeper and more meaningful life.

A Tale of Awakening

Four years ago, Tibetan Buddhist teacher, Mingyur Rinpoche, left a very comfortable position as the head of a monastery and quickly rising in popularity, due in part to a trio of books he released including *The Joy of Living*, to wander the Indian countryside in much the same way as the Hindu yogis once did.

This story fascinated me for some time and I closely followed it from the moment I found out about it. There was a time actually, the first and only time until he returned, where he was sighted. That was really exciting. I found it really admirable that he set off on such a journey despite his comfortable position. Not too long after that story posted, he resurfaced. Lionsroar.com, one of my favorite Buddhist publications on the internet, was able to get an exclusive interview with him, and there were a few really interesting moments, one of which I want to draw your attention to (for the full interview, visit lionsroar.com):

"What was the best experience you had?

It was actually a near-death experience I had in Kushinagar, the holy place where the Buddha died, not long after I started my retreat. I got very sick with vomiting and diarrhea, and one morning my health was so bad that I was sure I was going to die.

When I got sick, it felt like I went through some kind of wall of solid attachment to my body, my comfort, my robes, and even the idea of Mingyur Rinpoche. I slowly let go, let go, let go, let go. In the end, I even let go of myself. I thought, "If I'm going to die, okay. If I'm going to die, no problem." At that moment, I didn't have any fear.

I had some kind of dissolution, as they call it in the texts, and lost touch with my physical body altogether. Then I had a wonderful experience. There was no thought, no emotion, no concept, no subject or object. Mind was clear and wakeful, like a blue sky with the sun shining, transparent and all-pervasive. It's very, very difficult to describe. It cannot really be put into words.

And this is the result, his decision, based on that realization. How he's decided to change the way he teaches...

Now that you're back, how will this experience change the way you teach the dharma?

I want to teach in a more experiential style—not just meditation and practice, but also behavior and conduct. View, meditation, and conduct—these three together are very important. Maybe in the past I put more emphasis on view and meditation. Now I want to emphasize how meditation can transform our day-to-day life. Intellect, heart, and behavior—all three together.

I feel that happiness is really found in appreciation and rejoicing. Everything is a display of clarity, love, and wisdom. This is related to the main view of Vajrayana Buddhism: that we all are Buddha. This enlightened nature is not just within you. It's everywhere. You can see it and appreciate it. That's the main cause of happiness—gratitude and appreciation.

It's that near-death experience which has completely shifted his perspective, whether you'd call it full enlightenment, a moment of insight, or something else, and caused a great deal of gratitude and appreciation to arise within him. And it's this state of deep gratitude and appreciation- both just two shades of the same thing- which has liberated him. He goes on to say that he now feels as though he's a bird, completely free, able to fly wherever he'd like.

It's this point, of realizing the truth of our life, of our impermanence, and of the great gift that this life truly is, that I want to emphasize. However, not all of us go through near-death experiences. So, what are we supposed to do? How do we begin to work towards this realization? There are a number of practices and principles that will help us work through this. Simply working to be open to, and intently looking for in our daily lives, this truth of impermanence is a step in the right direction. Our mindfulness practice allows us to live fully awake to this moment, therefore being able to notice more clearly this truth at work in our lives and acknowledging it clearly when we see it arise. But I'd also like to talk about two powerful exercises for working through this challenging truth and seeing through to the true nature of things. The heart of this first exercise is the Buddha's *5 Daily Recollections*.

How to Practice: The Buddha's 5 Daily Recollections

The Buddha referred to the 5 Daily Recollections as "facts that everyone should reflect upon". These are facts of the highest regard, facts to live by. They're facts to structure our life around:

This Moment

1. *I'm of the nature to grow old. There is no way to escape growing old.*
2. *I am of the nature to have ill health. There is no way to escape having ill health.*
3. *I am of the nature to die. There is no way to escape death.*
4. *All that is dear to me and everything I have and everything I love are of the nature to change. There is no way to escape from losing them.*
5. *My actions are my only true belongings. I cannot escape the consequences of my actions. My actions are the ground on which I stand.*

Even after simply reading these, without taking any time to contemplate on each of them individually, I immediately feel a strong emotional reaction. Each of these facts is significant and compelling at the same time. They don't just hit you, and hit you hard, they *compel* you to take action. These 5 Daily Recollections are essentially all based on the single truth of impermanence looked at from various different angles and they can help you begin to cultivate a deep appreciation for life.

The exercise here is very simple:

Recite the 5 Daily Recollections once per day, taking a moment to contemplate on each before moving on to the next one.

This is a very simple daily practice that should only take somewhere between 2-5 minutes, but which can have a real impact on the way you live your life.

In the West, we shy from death. We do everything we can to either avoid it or beat it. In certain cultures, it's commonplace to contemplate on death and it's seen as highly beneficial to do so. It's no coincidence that these are either Eastern cultures or centrally Buddhist ones. To practice daily to face the fact of our own impermanence, and the impermanence of all that we care about, is a deeply nourishing exercise. And this practice is the very practice of waking up, because it's the realization of this deep state of appreciation which is a characteristic of awakening. This state of deep gratitude and appreciation is a state in which the lines have blurred and we're keenly aware of not just our own impermanence, but the way in which everything co-exists in every moment.

To be deeply aware of the truth of interbeing, of the fact that we are wholly dependent upon countless factors to not just be alive and healthy but to live the specific lifestyle we live now, is to realize a deep appreciation for everything around us. In this way, we realize that there is no separation between "you" and "I", "them" and "us", "me" and "that". But rather, that it's a complicated web of interbeing. This is what Alan Watts meant when he said, "You're it man". The self isn't me and then you, it's an interwoven tapestry. This tapestry expresses itself in myriad ways. An infinitely complicated expression. And to be one of those expressions is an incredible gift which we can't take for granted.

Don't waste this life – Realize the impermanent nature of all things

"Great is the matter of birth and death. All is impermanent, quickly passing. Wake up! Wake up, each one! Don't waste this life."

- Dogen Zenji

The "Great matter" he speaks of is this life. This life is birth and death. That's our life. The great matter is a central teaching in Buddhism and it's really just about the fact that this life is transitory, impermanent, and that we should strive diligently to understand it so that we can wake up and realize true peace.

Dogen is saying that there is something "more" out there, something "other" than what we experience as we trudge along with our normal lives without introspection, without contemplation or study of this life of ours, and that by doing so we can wake up to the beauty of our lives. So the effort isn't to figure out how to live as if we were going to die, to recreate this near-death experience, or the after-effects, it's to realize deeply that we are going to die. We're going to die. But this isn't contemplated on to be depressing, this is a fact. And because this is a fact, it needs to be transcended in order to realize true freedom. Facing this truth is the only way to overcome it. So, the point is to live knowing we're going to die and cultivating a deep appreciation for life as a result.

So we live as if we're going to die by being keenly aware of our impending death each and every day, and in this way, we awaken each morning with fresh lungs to receive the beauty and significance of each moment. This state of being allows us to appreciate even the simplest things in our everyday lives. We no longer strive for weighty accomplishments, at least for our own ego-based satisfaction. We're simply content as we are. If there is any striving done, it's to help others because we become so keenly aware of our connection with them and of their own impermanence along with our own.

Because of the impermanent nature of all things, we, as well as everyone and everything around us has a finite amount of time available in this life. It's because of this that we shouldn't waste a single moment of it.

How to Practice: Seeing Deeply

This Moment

With mindfulness and the practice of seeing deeply, a distinct form of contemplation, we can see into the impermanent nature of things and cultivate a sense of gratitude and appreciation for our life and the little moments. Smelling a flower, touching a tree, being with a loved one. In each of these moments, we can see clearly the impermanent nature of all things- both the moment and the things- and fully appreciate them for all their beauty:

1. Pick an object

This could be a flower, a tree, a piece of food, or even a person (although that's a bit of an advanced form of the practice). Whatever it is, pick one object and focus on that, preferably an organic object like a plant or some whole food.

2. Work backwards

Take a flower for instance. Start with where you got it- the store, flower shop, outside in your garden, at the park or wherever. Then imagine, or find out if you don't know, how it got to the flower shop, how it was transported, how it was maintained for freshness, how it was cared for and picked, and how it grew from a seed in the ground into a flower. Lastly, think about the soil and all the things that make up the soil that would eventually provide the seed the nutrients to grow into the flower as it sits in front of you now.

3. Realize interbeing

Lastly, think of how if you were to take away even one of those elements: the grower, the garden, the soil, the seed, or the facility that packaged and delivered it, the flower would cease to exist.

This Moment

This is a simple and easy meditation which you can do on just about anything, you just may have to stop to do a little searching to find out exactly where that thing comes from. But that can be an exciting and insightful exercise in itself (and something easily done nowadays with the internet). After practicing this a few times on a few different objects, do this on yourself and see the many different conditions which you do and have depended on to exist as you are today and see that even we don't escape this great truth of interbeing.

I'll leave you with these words from Zenkei Blanche Hartman, the former abbot of the San Francisco Zen Center. This is from her book, *Seeds from a Boundless Life*:

"In 1989 I had a heart attack. As I was leaving the hospital, I stepped out into the sunshine, and I had this sudden realization. "Wow! I'm alive. I could be dead. Wow, the rest of my life is just a gift." And then I thought, "Oh, it always has been, from the very beginning. Nobody owed me this life. It was just given to me. Wow!" And in that moment of waking up, I found what a wonderful, rich feeling it is to be grateful to be alive. Just right now, right here, all the time. I don't have to have anything more special than knowing that just to be alive is enough."

Holding on, Letting Go and the Seasons of Life

Life has varied seasons and moments in which different ways of being call upon us like a light wind seeks to wave a flag in the sky.

In many ways, the principle of resistance I spoke about at the beginning of Part III is a matter of holding on vs. letting go. Or rather, the ever-popular topic of letting go vs. holding on is a matter of understanding resistance. Here's a refresher on the principle of resistance:

We're resisting what is, to put it simply. There's really nothing more to it. This is the basic reason why we suffer in every way. We're fighting against the natural way of things instead of working to live in harmony.

When talking about the topics of when to let go, when to hold on, and *how* to let go when it sometimes seems impossible, it's this basic principle of resistance which we'll keep coming back to.

Holding On (Leaning in)

Clearly, letting go gets most of the attention. We're all too damned attached to everything that we generally don't feel there's an issue with our ability to hold on and because what we're really interested in is finding peace and freedom, letting go seems to be the ticket. However, it's more complicated than that.

Let's talk about holding on for a moment. What does holding on, attaching, to things actually look like in everyday life? Let's go over some examples:

- *A break up or divorce:* When one person just won't let the other person go and continues to be tortured by the person's absence.

- *Intimate love:* When one person has created an image in their mind of what their ideal partner should be or act like and perpetuates that image off onto their partner, instead of letting them freely be themselves.

- *Driving home from work:* When we drive home from work with the expectation that we'll get home without a hitch, but end up running into traffic and becoming very annoyed and angered as a result. That expectation we're holding on to is driving us to anger, not the reality of things.

- *Striving for success or greatness:* Living your life wanting to "get it all" for yourself, constantly trying to bend and rearrange things to get what you want. Ultimately, you're doing this to be at peace, but this isn't where true peace lies. Because this isn't the way things work, where true peace actually exists, you send yourself down a path of bad habits and patterns that fight against the true nature of things, leading to pain and suffering for you and often many other beings.

Ultimately, this is us clinging or attaching to certain ideas and expectations that just aren't true. And by clinging to these ideas and expectations we're resisting reality (or the true nature of things) and causing ourselves pain and suffering. This clearly demonstrates the importance of letting go. However, that's the easy one. It's not just about what we need to let go of, it's also about what we need to stop running from.

Moments in which we should rather be moving towards something, instead of letting go, come in a much subtler form. Since we were little, many of us have been taught to distract ourselves from our problems as opposed to facing them. This behavior stays with us to adulthood and we end up living our lives doing everything we can to avoid our problems. We...

- *Eat*
- *Drink*
- *Smoke*
- *Have sex*
- *Play games*
- *Surf online*
- *Watch T.V.*
- *Engage in groups that help justify our actions*
- *And so much more...*

...All because we've been conditioned that the only way to get away from our problems is to push them away or bottle them down, essentially drowning them (and ourselves) in patterns of unwholesome behavior. Keep in mind, almost none of these behaviors are bad in-and-of-themselves, they're bad when used as a way to avoid our problems and difficulties. But the reality is, you'll never overcome your problems and realize peace and freedom unless you summon the courage to face those problems and lean in to them. This can be very difficult to do, but it's absolutely worth it. The practice of facing or leaning into our challenges, our suffering, so that we can be with it in mindfulness, compassion, and loving-kindness is an act of holding on. We much rather push these things away, but it's only by leaning in to them that we can create healing. In many ways it is leaning in, but it's also holding on because while we experience this suffering head-on we have to make the intentional effort to stay with it. Of course, holding on has a bit of a wrong connotation with regards to the practice as a whole. Leaning in is much more accurate for expressing the action itself that needs to be taken.

Keep in mind as well that it's by facing our harmful patterns of behavior- the act of pushing away- that we have the ability to let go of the pain that exists beneath the surface, so it's more of a dance of holding on and then letting go at different moments than it is holding on vs. letting go. Everything is connected in this way and so the act of separating things in any way is a misunderstanding (at least in actual practice and comprehension).

How to Practice: A Mindful Welcome

A Mindful Welcome is about welcoming difficult thoughts, emotions, and sensations with the healing energy of mindfulness. It's about the fundamental shift from "hostile enemy" to "welcoming friend" we must make to begin on the path to healing. This is the practice of leaning in.

1. Sit with the difficulty

This meditation is done in the midst of the arising of difficult thoughts, emotions, or sensations. When you experience something arising, either spontaneously or due to a recent occurrence (an argument, tragic news, an unwelcomed surprise), find a quiet (or at least secluded) place to stand or sit. Begin first by acknowledging the thought, feeling, sensation or combination of thoughts, feelings, and sensations within you. Imagine that you are having a house party and are preparing for your guests to arrive.

2. Become aware of your breath

Simply turn your attention to your breathing. Follow each in-breath and out-breath from beginning to end. Place a firm, but soft, focus on the breath.

3. Welcome (acknowledge openly) the challenge 5 times

Various thoughts, feelings, and sensations will arise while being mindful and, as a result, you will lose your concentration on the breath. As usual, acknowledge them and then return to your breath. In this meditation, though, you're making a special effort to acknowledge the particular thoughts, feelings, and sensations associated with this difficulty in a very particular way.

Imagine that you're opening the door to your home and welcoming this difficulty fully with all of your being in an act of love and compassion. When you notice the difficulty arise, in whatever form it takes (thought, feeling, sensation), take a moment to hold onto it and imagine greeting it with a feeling of love and caring.

4. Return to being mindful of the breath

Return to the breath as many times as is necessary until you have acknowledged the difficulty arise on five separate occasions. Then, allow yourself to rise slowly and mindfully and continue on with your day.

Letting Go

You've probably seen or read something like it before on the Internet. A beautiful image with a short quote that says something to the significance of "let it go" (if you don't believe me, type "let go" into Google and look under the images tab). And I'm not talking about the Frozen theme song, I'm talking about the idea of letting go of things in your life, whatever that may be. But rarely is it explained how to actually "let it go". More often than not it's become no more than a slogan for happy living, with vague guidance at best (like "be yourself"). What I do find interesting, though, is that most of us seem to realize intuitively how important it is to live without clinging, even if we're not exactly sure how that's supposed to happen (once again, like *be yourself*).

However, there's a vast amount of wisdom in Eastern thought that can help us learn how to let go of the many things which bind us and keep us from finding peace and freedom. That's where the teaching on non-attachment comes in. The teaching on non-attachment, as described in Buddhist and Hindu thought, is often misunderstood- especially in the West. It's usually misunderstood as the detaching from all worldly things in a physical sense, which most of us aren't all that interested in doing (and also, intuitively, feel is unnecessary). The common image of a yogi living and meditating in a cave doesn't help that misconception either.

In fact, when Buddhism first came to China somewhere around 2,000 years ago by way of these reclusive and hermit-like practicing Buddhists, the Chinese apparently didn't dig it all that much either. They didn't see the point of removing yourself entirely from worldly activities and becoming these sort of recluses from society. But they were very much interested in Buddhism in general and would go on to spur one of the most significant reforms in Buddhist history- the birth of what's called "Mahayana" (or "the great vehicle") Buddhism.

The reason I mention this story is to illustrate why it can be so dang confusing to understand what's meant by non-attachment in ancient Eastern thought. This is because technically there is a side of Buddhism that's about becoming that mountain recluse or hermit and living by yourself for the rest of your life. Fortunately, the Chinese realized the truth early on that such a way of living only aided in the path to realizing peace and was in no way a requirement. The truth is peace and freedom can be obtained right here within everyday life. So then, if stripping yourself of all possessions and worldly responsibility isn't the point of non-attachment, *what is*?

What is Non-Attachment?

The Buddhist teaching on non-attachment is ultimately about realizing the truth of yourself. That is, realizing that you're an expression of everything. That you're in the cosmos, that the entire cosmos is in you in a very real and observable way, and that there is no separating the two (and everything that comes with that realization). And the teaching on non-attachment is about living in such a way that you live without such obstructions that keep you from realizing this.

So, for instance, it's not about not being able to get married, something which Chinese Buddhists began allowing which Indian Buddhists didn't, it's about not attaching yourself to your spouse or the concept of marriage in a particular way. This means living in a way that instead of keeping this image of your spouse in your mind and falling in love with that image, consequently running into problems when that image changes, you let them free and accept them fully for who they are in each moment no matter what changes. In Zen Buddhism, when students complete their study they're allowed to enter back into a "normal" life and do things such as marry and take jobs. This is because it's understood in Zen that non-attachment isn't about physical items, locations, and such, it's about the ideas we occupy our minds with. It's about what we believe about ourselves and the world around us. This means that you could lead a perfectly normal life on the surface, but from within live in a way that you don't attach yourself to any of the things that are a part of your life. This doesn't mean you stop caring about them, on the contrary you appreciate them so much more because you're ever-aware of the fact that they won't be around (at least in this form) forever.

So, just as you can hold a flower in your hand, being well aware that the flower will wilt and die in a matter of days, taking in the smell and beauty of the flower, you can live your entire life savoring every moment knowing that in each moment everything can (and often does) change and being open and ready for when change occurs.

How We Attach in Our Everyday Life

Any belief that you're this separate entity which exists detached from the rest of existence, and your attempts to cling to these ideas as well as your attempts to cling to expectations about the way the world is supposed to work, cause friction between yourself and the rest of the interconnected world and result in pain and the inability for you to find peace. Remember, ultimately, it all comes back to the principle of resistance.

However, what does this look like in your everyday life? Putting aside all the cosmos this and interconnected that talk, how can we begin to notice this in our daily lives? When it comes down to it, all attachment originates with the ego

This Moment

(there's that ego again). The ego, a construct which was built through years of conditioning and is in no way a "real" part of you at all, is what convinces you that you're this separate entity disconnected from all other living and non-living things. Your ego is an image, it's who you believe yourself to be. And when reality doesn't match up to the image, friction happens and pain occurs. Pain caused by your attachment to the ego could come from:

- Not hitting your personal performance goals at work, leading you to question if your abilities are declining.

- Not performing as well during a basketball game with some old friends as you used to when you were younger, realizing you're not as fit as you used to be and maybe no longer the athlete you thought yourself as.

- Finding out your spouse cheated on you and your dream of having a family and living the rest of your life with this great person consequently shattering.

Also, when life doesn't = your expectations, the same happens:

- Losing a loved one and having to come to grips with the fact that this person who meant so much to you and who you're used to having in your life is gone forever.

- Being fired from the job you've had for the past ten years and thought you'd spend the rest of your life at.

- A co-worker whom you trusted stabbing you in the back to win a promotion over you.

To see this more clearly, think about something that doesn't surprise you. Think about a sandwich. Let's say you really like peanut butter and jelly sandwiches and you're used to having one every afternoon for lunch.

Provided everything goes as normal, you enjoy your sandwich and have a pleasant lunch. But, if it turns out your husband or wife pranked you and threw some soy sauce in there when they made your sandwich (no wonder they offered to make it today...), you wouldn't have a very pleasant lunch. The surprise of the PB&J not adding up to your expectation is what caused you the pain, not that soy sauce was in it.

If you were to have eaten that sandwich like you had never had a peanut butter sandwich before in your life, without expectations, not only would the real thing have tasted better, experiencing every bite like the first time, but you wouldn't have been disappointed when you were pranked with the PB&JS (peanut butter and jelly-soy) your spouse made for you because you would have had no expectation of how it should taste.

How to Let Go

The same basic ingredients apply in all forms of letting go, but there's multiple ways to begin the process. One very important point I want to mention with regards to the entire subject, though, is to not attach yourself to any one method of letting go.

It sounds odd that you can find a new attachment through trying to let go of all attachments, but it's a very real thing to look out for. Don't get mixed up thinking the finger pointing the way to the moon is the moon itself. What this means is, first and foremost, non-attachment is a state of mind. New attachments will always threaten you, so to live with the state of mind of non-attachment, to realize the importance of living in a way that you go with the natural flow of things (living naturally) and respect the impermanence of all life, is the basis for realizing non-attachment.

Again, there's many ways to go about it, but the first step is generally to begin working to identify the ego, which will come from dedication to your mindfulness and meditation practice. This can take time, and can be challenging, but the process itself is very rewarding. To strive to live with mindfulness in each moment, whether you're sitting on the meditation cushion, walking from one place to the next, or are at work, is to shine a light on your entire life and uncover the presence of the ego in each area of your life, even the furthest reaches that lay hidden deep in your subconscious. To live with mindfulness is also to live fully engaged and yet unattached in that very moment. To be mindful is to be open and accepting of whatever may come in any moment, so mindfulness is a multipurpose tool in letting go of the many attachments we hold.

There's another way to help us let go in our everyday life, though. To look deeply at those things in our everyday life, especially ourselves, is to realize not only the interconnected nature of all things as we discussed earlier but also the impermanence. We discussed impermanence in detail in the last chapter, but there's an effective meditation practice on impermanence we can use that's particularly effective at helping us let go of attachments.

How to Practice: Meditating on the End of Your Life

Meditating on death sounded like a bit of a harsh title, but that's essentially what this meditation is about. Keep in mind, you don't have to go too deep here. If you do choose to do so though, be careful, you might not like everything you find (which is the same in all forms of meditation, but especially so for this). Regardless, this is a very healing meditation. This is very much a different shade of the Seeing Deeply contemplation exercise we covered in the last chapter.

To meditate on death, simply imagine it's your time and everything that will come with it. You could be on a hospital bed, your personal bed, or somewhere else. For best effect, imagine the process is pretty far along, and you've been looking back on your life. You'll likely have to sit with this exercise for some time before things begin coming to the surface, but they will come. Maybe you begin seeing flashes of your daughter, who you've fought with for years, come into your mind. You won't always know why, but by focusing your mind on this near-death event certain things will arise naturally. After some time, imagine that you have passed. Picture yourself in the ground (or wherever you'll be) and imagine the way that life will go on without you- your family, friends, and the world.

Part of this process can be active with contemplation, trying to actively imagine what kinds of things you might regret, wished you'd have done differently, or feel relieved you can finally let go of, and another part more passive by simply thinking about the situation to yourself for a moment and then proceeding to sit and follow your breath with mindfulness and accepting whatever thoughts arise as a part of that.

No matter how you decide to practice this meditation, meditating on the end of your life, can be a powerful and insightful exercise in the practice of letting go of attachments.

Seasons of Life

The principles of leaning in and letting go are paramount in the practice of living naturally. However, as I mentioned earlier, it's not so simple. To say holding on vs. letting go is to draw too big of a distinction on a thing which is

This Moment

constantly moving and constantly changing in every moment. For this, the metaphor *seasons of life* is much more sensible.

Seasons of life is a metaphor for life. Just as there are four seasons: summer, fall, winter, and spring there are seasons of life or moments in life where various perspectives are most harmonious with the state of our life. These are the seasons of our life:

During Winter, the flowers are barren and the trees lonely. They work to preserve themselves in preparation for another Spring. During this time, we must be present for our suffering and rest in the healing power of sorrow and sadness.

During Spring, the flowers once again bloom, the trees spring back to life and what was once on the brink of life now comes back in full color and vibrancy. During this time, the natural season of life calls us to renew ourselves and start anew.

During Summer, the flowers, trees, and life flourish. Too much sunlight can be bad, but for the most part, this is a good time which should be appreciated and enjoyed fully. During this time, we must open ourselves to the moment and hold on to what we love, nourishing it and giving it our full attention.

During Fall, the flowers wilt and the leaves fall, leaving barren and lonely trees. Life turns inward and attends to itself. During this time, we must learn to let go, see deeply, and accept change as a natural part of life.

To simplify life down to holding on, or leaning in, vs. letting go is a damaging oversimplification. Life has varied seasons and moments in which different ways of being call upon us like a light wind seeks to wave a flag in the sky. By learning to pay attention to our mind and our body in a careful

This Moment

and caring way, we can sense these seasons and move throughout life in a more peaceful and harmonious way.

This Moment

Part IV: Living Lovingly

This Moment

True Love & Our Search for Meaning

There's a deep current that runs throughout this world, but most of us have become numb to it. That current is love.

When I was in eighth grade, I wrote a letter to a girl in my school. We'll call her Vanessa. I did so because I was too shy to ask her to be my girlfriend. I know, quite the gentleman, right? Sarcasm aside, to my surprise, she said yes. From that moment on, and for the next 9 months, we became almost inseparable. Eighth grade marked the completion of middle school for us and the following year we would go on to the same high school together. In between that, Summer.

For the first month or so, Vanessa and I spent nearly every day together. It was an amazing time marked with total infatuation for one another and all to ourselves. However, by the time Summer came to an end, my world had come shattering down around me and I felt as if the very ground I walked on was shaky, at best.

One month into the Summer, she took a planned trip with her family to Mexico that lasted about one month. While on that trip, she spent most of her time with a boy she had met. Let's call him Scott (I know, great choice in names). Long story short, after a patchy few months we eventually broke up

This Moment

just after beginning as Freshman in high school. The honeymoon was over and I was left wounded for what felt like (and probably was) years.

This might have been my story, but most of us have a story just like it. However, that wasn't a story about love. It was a story about the void that dictates so much of our lives. It was a story about two people coming together with mutual fantasies about finding "the one" and being completed. It was a story about two people desperately trying to fill the void they each felt within their hearts, without having any knowledge of how to do it. When you place all of your hopes and expectations- the fantasy- on another person like that, you're asking for trouble. Once you, or the other person, realizes that they won't get what they want, they leave and go somewhere else- wherever they believe they can go to fill the void in their hearts.

There's a deep current that runs throughout this world, but most of us have become numb to it. That current is love. Unfortunately, most of us have floated off into a place of fear, lack, and as I often refer to it: the feeling that "something" is missing (the void).

We search for meaning outside ourselves in many different ways:

- *We seek to feel "complete" through intimate relationships.*
- *We seek to feel fulfilled through big accomplishments.*
- *We seek to feel loved through sex.*
- *And we seek to feel content through harmful, unhealthy, or generally neutral repetitive activities (this takes shape in many ways).*

However it is that we act out this basic human illness, it's all towards the same purpose of making ourselves "full"- to fill that sense of voidness within us and, unknowingly, get back to the current of love. Unfortunately, most of us go about it the wrong way and end up hurting ourselves more than anything else. To walk this journey to ourselves, more is necessary than just mindfulness, intentional living, and the ability to more skillfully navigate the great challenges we covered in Part III. We need love- *true* love. Not only for others, but for ourselves.

So far, in *This Moment*, we've discussed:

1. *Living mindfully:* We learned about the power of mindfulness, how to approach the practice, individual practices, making mindfulness a way of life, and we learned about the path to making friends with ourselves. Here, we established the foundation of our practice.

2. *Living intentionally:* We established a basic perspective as well as a framework for living more intentionally, learned how to consume mindfully and tend to the garden of our consciousness, focused our efforts by learning to live with a more one-pointed mind, further simplified our life, and established the right effort conducive to an effective practice and greater peace and freedom. Here, we established a container for our practice which made our practice more effective and ourselves calmer and more at peace.

3. *Living naturally:* We learned the underlying factor which leads to so much pain and suffering and how to instead open ourselves fully to each moment, how to express ourselves truly and naturally, how to deepen our daily experience and live with a sense of appreciation by facing the truth of impermanence, and how to walk the seasons of life including leaning in and letting go. Here, we leaned in to

This Moment

many of the most fundamental challenges of this life and learned how to live more skillfully.

We've covered quite a bit so far. Some might even wonder what is really left to be said. The truth is, while each other part of the book is, in a way, supporting *Living Mindfully,* you could also make a case for Part IV being the most important part and principle of all. Part IV is, simply, about love. However, I don't mean just intimate love, or even the love you feel for your family and friends. The love I speak of has no boundaries, so to confine it to something like intimate love or love for a friend or family member, or even all of the above, is to confine its limitless power and significance. In the scope of the book so far, without Part IV: *Living Lovingly,* the book would lack heart (pun intended). By that I mean that basic human quality would be altogether missing. When we practice mindfulness and meditation, we encounter all kinds of different thoughts and feelings that range from slightly uncomfortable to potentially traumatic. This is the journey to yourself that we spoke about earlier. Without *true* love and its accompanying qualities- compassion, loving-kindness, joy, and equanimity (or freedom), we would be without some of the most critical tools necessary for navigating life's challenges. And we'd be altogether cut off from the basic current that connects us all and gives us the ability to relieve others suffering.

In Part IV, I'll explain the teaching on true love that came to us thousands of years ago from the Brahmin's of ancient India, why it's so important, and its connection to our search for peace and freedom. We'll talk about how to cultivate the critical qualities of loving-kindness and compassion and overall how to live in a more loving way with yourself, those around you, and the world at large both in formal and informal meditative practice. We'll also talk about finding ourselves in love, be it intimate love, family, or friendship and the importance of freedom. And, lastly, we'll talk about opening up the mind to the ultimate truth of our interbeing, interconnected, nature and encompassing the world with great love and compassion.

What is True Love?

For most of us, the story I illustrated at the beginning of this chapter is what we think of when we imagine love (or, at least, without the crashing and burning part. Well, maybe.). We believe that true love is the highest level of intimate love, or all of love for that matter. This is the point of intimate relationships, dating, and everything else in between. The word love connotes intimate love and often nothing else, possibly including the love we have for friends and family. Although, save for our children, we still hold intimate love on a pedestal even when compared to that.

That is love, or at least it can be, but it's only a small part of it. Our intense obsession with intimate love, especially in the West (although this is true everywhere), is about the void we feel in our hearts. This void is in fact the absence of love, but love itself isn't something given to us. Love is something which we have the capacity for within ourselves. For this reason, any searching outside ourselves for love is a misguided effort, whether it be through intimate love or the desire to have children (for that specific reason). So then, what exactly is real true love? It's important that before we move on we're clear on what real love is.

In my first book, *The Little Book of Mindfulness*, I spoke briefly about how the Buddha was excellent at speaking to others through the light of their own spiritual tradition. I think the Buddha had a keen ability to distill the wisdom from the ancient traditions which existed around ancient India at the time and he used this ability skillfully. I say this, partly, because he adapted what was often called the "Four Immeasurables" from the Brahmins in his own teaching. At the time in ancient India there was quite a lot of change occurring all around the country and the more I study the more I see that the popularity of the Buddha's teachings were partly due to this huge shift that was happening in India at the time. There was a lot of unrest then, which suggests they were in the "Winter & Spring" season of life as I mentioned at the end of Part III, where what is has become withered and morphed and there must be a cleansing and revitalizing of life to bring back the old wisdom. Well, the four immeasurables were a part of that revitalized wisdom.

The four immeasurables go by another name, though: the *four aspects of true love*. These four aspects are the definition of true love in Buddhist wisdom. As I spoke briefly about in the introduction, the four aspects of true love are:

1. *Loving*-Kindness: Loving-kindness is our capacity to care for and give kindness and happiness to others.
2. *Compassion*: Compassion is our capacity to feel the suffering of others. But more so than just that, this aspect is also the desire to relieve suffering.
3. *Sympathetic Joy*: By sympathetic joy, I mean a joy characterized by the ability to rejoice in the happiness, well-being, and good fortune of others.
4. *Equanimity*: This could also be referred to as freedom, because equanimity refers to treating others equally and not clinging or attaching.

It's these four qualities which are the essence of true love. To love someone truly is to have each one of these four qualities present at all times. To love someone truly means you care for them and have the capacity to give them happiness. It means you can feel their pain and that you have a desire to relieve their suffering. It means you can rejoice in their happiness and truly feel happy for them, even when there is nothing in it for you. And, lastly, to love someone truly means you allow them to be free, to be themselves, allowing them to stretch their wings wherever they will go without a sense of clinging.

Throughout Part IV, we'll be exploring true love and discussing how to apply these principles in practical ways to living more fully and freely in the present moment (and helping others do the same).

The Power of True Love

Now, at this point, you may be wondering what this has to do with the practice we've been outlining thus far. Love, in the Western sense at least, is always between two people, so how does this come into the picture? To be sure, knowing how to properly love others already reliefs much pain and suffering and gives us the ability to cultivate a great deal of peace and happiness. However, these qualities don't just have to do with others, they apply directly to how we treat ourselves as well. As I mentioned in the introduction:

...We love ourselves in either a free and open way, or in a confining and critical way.
...We love ourselves in either a joyous way, rejoicing in our good fortune and successes, or constantly beating ourselves up and always telling ourselves we're not good enough.
...We love ourselves in either a compassionate way, taking care of ourselves when we experience some pain or suffering, or in a neglectful way, ignoring our needs and never really doing what's necessary to take care of ourselves.
...and we love ourselves in either a kind and caring way, being kind to ourselves when we suffer a setback, failure, internal or external criticism, or suffering of any other kind, or in an unkind way, always talking down to ourselves and making ourselves suffer due to actions against ourselves.

This Moment

These four qualities of true love are valuable tools in the practice of making friends with yourself. Without loving-kindness, compassion, joy, and freedom we would be incapable of walking the path effectively. To live fully and freely in each moment is to lean in and face our challenges. And to face our challenges effectively is to have the capacity to love ourselves as well as others. However, there's much more to it than just giving us valuable tools for facing our challenges.

When we lack love, we're shut off from ourselves and the world around us. This is because *understanding is the basis for love*. This can't be understated. In many ways, understanding is love. There's a clear and direct connection between the two. To understand ourselves is to have love and compassion for ourselves. And to understand ourselves is to live with greater peace and joy and to better navigate life's challenges. And understanding others relieves much suffering in us and gives us the ability to relieve the suffering of others as well. Every one of these things helps us in our effort to live more fully and freely in the present moment.

Also, in many ways, love is the ultimate reference point for spiritual practice. Love is the one unifying factor across essentially all spiritual and religious traditions, to the point where it's almost unbelievable. The reason for this is that love is the energy which binds us. In true love, two people become one. Their suffering becomes our suffering. Our suffering becomes theirs. And their happiness becomes ours, and ours theirs, as well. It is in true love that we can see the principle of interbeing in action. Interbeing is a basic element of our existence. It tells the story of our origin and existence. In every moment, each and every thing in this world is made up of elements which are not its own (or, at least, not exclusively its own).

An apple, for instance, is made up of all non-apple elements. The dirt, the rain, the clouds that provided the rain,

This Moment

the sunlight, the apple tree, and even the farmer that grew the apple tree. If you look closely at anything you'll see that it's made up of elements which are not its own, connecting it in countless ways to the rest of the world. In this way, the apple is *interbeing* in every moment with the world around it. In the same way that the apple exists, so do we. And one of the ways this manifests most significantly in our lives is through love, the process of bringing two people together as one, interbeing with one another in numerous ways. In the interbeing of love, I am made up of the suffering of my wife and children. I am also made up of the happiness of my wife and children as well. I am made up of countless non-me elements in each and every moment. This then expands out from us to one other person to all beings at the height of love.

And, lastly, love is what allows us to fill the "void" in our hearts. As we spoke about in the beginning of this chapter, it's love which sends us on a wild goose chase throughout life, trying hopelessly to fill this space with intimate love, sex, power, fame, and just about anything else. But each and every one of these efforts misses the mark because love is a capacity that exists within us, not something to be acquired outside.

Being Love

Love is a capacity which we hold innately within ourselves in each and every moment.

All our lives, we've been taught that love is something acquired. Love is something which is given to us by our mother, our father, our grand parents, and let's not forget, our *one true love*. Intuitively, we know the importance of love, at least to some degree. Because of this, if we don't receive it at home we go out searching for it in the world around us. This lack of love growing up can lead to all kinds of deep issues that make us feel inadequate and worthless. Sometimes, this can even manifest in the form of damaging patterns such as an addiction to sex. Have you ever known someone who seemed to be incapable of going a week without being in a relationship? As soon as they would break up with someone they'd almost immediately get together with someone else? They're starving for love (and, consequently, lacking self-worth) and get by with temporary infatuation and personal attention. It's all an effort to fill the void we feel in our hearts. But what if love *wasn't* something given to us? What if it was an ability that existed within us? How would that change the way you live your life? For most of us, it would be nothing short of a revolution. But this isn't some fantasy. This is reality.

This Moment

Love is a capacity which we hold innately within ourselves in each and every moment. The capacity to love exists within us. In other words, we create love. Or, perhaps more accurately, love is an opening up of the mind. By opening ourselves up we clear the once clogged pathway and can receive love from the deepest reaches of our being in each moment, not just from some specific person, but all people and all things.

By cultivating the ability to open this pathway and live openly in this way, we live grounded in the power of love. We have the power, in each moment of practice, to draw upon the power of loving-kindness and compassion to help heal internal wounds. Intimate love is a truly beautiful part of life (now we can discern true love from false love), the love our parents feel for us is as warm as ever, the love we feel for each one of the people in our life is sweeter than ever, and perhaps most importantly we now have a great deal of self-love. But, even more than that, we've now begun to open ourselves up to the basic energy of this deep connection we share and the deeply connected nature of all things.

Love is cultivated within you. It is your greatest asset and our greatest gift. So then, how do we go from a place of lacking love to a clear and open pathway which can not just generate self-love, but which can openly love others as well? For that, we must learn how to walk the path of love in meditation practice.

Walking the Path of Love

"Love is the capacity to take care, to protect, to nourish. If you are not capable of generating that kind of energy toward yourself- if you are not capable of taking care of yourself, of nourishing yourself, of protecting yourself- it is very difficult to take care of another person. In the Buddhist teaching, it's

clear that to love oneself is the foundation of the love of other people. Love is a practice. Love is truly a practice."

- Thich Nhat Hanh

Like a muscle, love can be strengthened with practice. We can develop our capacity to love, our capacity for compassion and loving-kindness, sympathetic joy, and equanimity, and in doing so, realize greater peace and freedom. The rest of this chapter will explore practical and effective practices for cultivating the qualities of loving-kindness, compassion, sympathetic joy, and equanimity both as a formal meditative practice and as informal "everyday" practices.

Loving-Kindness Meditation

The practice of loving-kindness, or metta/maitri (Pali/Sanskrit for love or kindness), meditation is a formal meditation practice which has been passed down since the time of the Buddha over 2,500 years ago. Loving-kindness meditation, or "LKM" for short, is about opening up the heart and cultivating love and compassion for ourselves and others. This is the most fundamental of all love-based meditative practices.

Today, we're very fortunate to have an asset such as the internet with which to communicate long-held wisdom and knowledge. If it weren't for that, these practices wouldn't be so easily accessible. If we look to Buddhist wisdom we see an unbroken lineage of practitioners, from the Buddha all the way to the present-day Dalai Lama, who have used loving-kindness meditation to transform their mind, open up their heart, and realize the way. This is the path to peace, freedom, and happiness through opening up to the current of love.

You'll notice in the instructions below that the very first thing you do in loving-kindness meditation is work on cultivating love for yourself. This is because it's through loving ourselves that we're able to love others. If we ignore our own well-being, our own peace and happiness, we're no good to anyone. When we nurture our mind we become a limitless beacon of light for others to feed off of, and in this way our peace and happiness helps others find peace and happiness as well.

How to Practice: Loving-Kindness Meditation

The practice of loving-kindness meditation is very easy to do and can be modified based on your preferences. The general idea behind loving-kindness meditation is that you're sending well-wishes, or positive thoughts, to yourself and others. I'd suggest starting with a mantra such as this:

May they be well. May they be happy.
May they be healthy. May they be at peace.
May they be free from pain and suffering.

Once you've practiced this for some time and have gotten used to the meditation itself, you can try different ways of practicing to find what is most comfortable and effective for you. You could:

- *Picture beautiful imagery to instill a sense of love and peace within you. You could imagine the person smiling at you.*
- *Chant simple phrases, like the mantra I listed above.*
- *Or simply say the mantra to yourself in your mind.*

This Moment

Loving-kindness meditation is essentially the practice of sending love to various people in different stages. You begin by generating love for yourself and then move on to the next down the line, passing this energy of love from one person to the next, eventually expanding this love to encompass all beings.

1. *First: Yourself*
2. *Second: A respected person/someone who has deeply cared for you.*
3. *Third: A friend or family member. Not so much on the second level, but still someone in your life that you care for.*
4. *Fourth: Someone neutral. Think random people you pass by in the store whom you've never met.*
5. *Fifth: Someone you dislike or hate. This could be anyone who has caused you suffering.*
6. *Sixth: All beings. Expand the feelings you've generated thus far outwardly to all beings.*

Now that we have that established, here are the instructions for practicing loving-kindness meditation. Remember, your doing each of the three steps below for each stage (you, a respected/beloved, etc.):

1. Hold an image of the person in your mind (<30 seconds)

Make this image as clear as possible and feel your connection with the person. Nothing specific is necessary here, just do your best to get a picture of the person in your mind that you can work with. For yourself, I suggest picturing yourself in your mind as clearly as you can just as the other stages, almost as if you're looking in the mirror.

2. Generate feelings of love for the person (3-5 minutes)

Say this or a similar mantra to yourself a few times in a row:

May they be well. May they be happy.
May they be healthy. May they be at peace.
May they be free from pain and suffering.

While you repeat this mantra, be fully present for each word. Feel each word fully and continue to hold the picture of the given person in your mind. Imagine this energy of love growing. If you become distracted during the meditation, simply bring yourself back to the mantra (there is a mindful aspect to loving-kindness meditation as well).

3. Imagine transferring those feelings of love to the next person (<30 seconds)

Let those feelings swell as high as they will go and then imagine you transferring that energy of love to the person in the following stage. If you just cultivated love for yourself, now imagine sending those feelings of love to your deeply respected or beloved one.

Once you get to the end and have cultivated love for each of these people, imagine everyone surrounding this energy of love and allowing it to expand out to encompass all of you (this includes yourself). Then, imagine this love expanding out to your city, your country, the world, and all beings in existence.

Some Final Tips

Here are a few important points with regards to loving-kindness meditation that should help you in the beginning of your practice:

1. Sending love to yourself may feel awkward

If sending love to yourself feels awkward, don't worry, you're not alone. This is natural and you may experience it. If that's the case, you can switch the first and second stage so that you're first cultivating love for a respected or beloved person and then sending those feelings to yourself, a close family member or friend, and on just as before. This is an effective way to practice in the beginning if you're having trouble.

2. You may not have a person to fulfill every stage

If that's the case, it's perfectly fine. There are only a few hard rules with this meditation, and having someone for each stage isn't one of them. If you can't particularly think of someone you dislike, think of someone who has annoyed you in the past and cultivate love for them, or skip the step so long as you have no one you can think of to fulfill the stage (but do your best to fulfill it. We pretty much all have someone we can use for each stage).

3. Practice makes perfect

Not perfect with regards to your skill level, but perfect with regards to your comfort level and the effectiveness of the meditation for you. Try out picturing imagery, chanting, and repeating to yourself internally to see what works best for you. Also try different mantras, mix in wording that compels feelings of love from you, and try different imagery if you're going that route.

Loving-kindness meditation can also be a very effective "everyday" practice as well for overcoming difficult daily challenges, which we'll talk about in the beginning of the next section.

Walking the Path of Love in Everyday Life

Loving-kindness meditation is the most well-known and most commonly used love-based meditative practice, but there's more to this practice than just the formal side of things. Just as in mindfulness practice, we can work to cultivate love throughout our everyday life in various ways. In this section, we'll cover a number of powerful practices for walking the path of love in day-to-day life.

1. Mindfulness and Self-Love

Before we move on to the major practices, I wanted to make sure and mention a very important practice in the path to cultivating true love. Cultivating self-love is very much about gaining clarity about what goes on within your mind, so it's important to mention that mindfulness and meditation is an important aspect of cultivating self-love.

By dedicating ourselves to our mindfulness practice, we can not only unearth difficult challenges which harm our self-worth and "block" us from within, allowing us to send love to ourselves and heal the wound, we also gain the ability to generate moments of happiness for ourselves all throughout the day. And, when we have a way to cultivate such moments of joy, we can transfer those feelings to our loved ones and help them experience a taste of true love as well.

2. Everyday Loving-Kindness

As we spoke about a moment ago, loving-kindness meditation is a formal meditation practice, but I've also adapted an "everyday" version of the practice for use when you're out and about and encounter difficult situations within yourself or between another.

Life is a mixture of so many different things. Sometimes it's great- peaceful, joyful, and quiet- other times it's crazy, hectic, overwhelming, or even downright brutal. When things get rough, we need to turn our attention inward for a moment and send loving-kindness and compassion our way. And this is where this simple meditation really shines.

How to Practice: Everyday Loving-Kindness

Before you start, ask yourself: is this an internal challenge (dealing only with me), or an internal-external challenge (a problem which has to do with me + others)? I'll explain why in a bit.

To practice Everyday Loving-Kindness, follow these simple instructions (3-4 minutes total):

1. Calm (1 minute)

Whatever the challenge, the first thing you should do is take a second to calm yourself. Become aware of your breath for a few moments and then repeat a simple mantra such as this to yourself for no more than a minute: "Be free. Be at peace."

2. Generate love (1 minute)

Next, imagine a close friend, family member, or mentor/teacher which you have a great deal of love for (and preferably respect, if possible). Keep an image of them in your mind for a minute and imagine those feelings of love and compassion for the person swelling up as high as they will go.

3. Send love to yourself (1 minute)

Now, imagine transferring those feelings of love and compassion for the person over to yourself. After doing so for a moment, you can repeat this mantra to yourself: "Be kind. Be compassionate. Be loving." Imagine transferring those feelings to yourself.

If this is an internal challenge, you can stop here. If this is an internal-external challenge, such as a recent fight with your spouse or conflict with your boss, do step four:

4. Send love to the other (1 minute)

Lastly, do the exact same thing as in the last step except send those feelings of love from yourself to the person who you've conflicted with (whether directly or simply mentally, such as when you notice having envy or jealously for another).

I've kept the practice period for the meditation very short so that it's extremely easy and convenient to practice within your everyday life, but you can lengthen each section if you'd like to practice longer.

When to use Everyday Loving-Kindness

When is Everyday Loving-Kindness useful? Its usefulness is endless, but here are some great examples of ways you can use this simple meditation to bring peace and balance to your daily life and help overcome daily challenges, both internal and external:

- *You were fired from your job, failed an exam, or didn't make the cut.* Practice sending compassion and love to yourself and remind yourself not only that you're human, but that things can't always work out how you imagine them (which doesn't mean this is bad- you never know what's around the corner).

- *You had a bad fight with a friend or family member.* This is not only difficult for both people internally, but creates a lot of external tension. By meditating on love and compassion, you can forgive yourself and the other person and encourage yourself to apologize, which more often than not leads the other person to open up and apologize as well. And this is very healing.

- *An expectation wasn't met, however small.* In everyday life, we fill ourselves up with expectations. This includes everything big and small from how the next year of our lives will go to whether our dog will pee on the bed again or not. By learning to identify this expectation as well as send love and compassion to yourself and anyone else involved, you can help dissolve the pain of the situation into peace.

There's so many examples of ways you can use Everyday Loving-Kindness to help you work through personal challenges, challenges between others, and other challenges dealing with the unfolding of everyday events. Everyday Loving-Kindness is a valuable tool which you can use when you encounter a difficult patch in your everyday life.

3. Healing Through Understanding

"The essence of love and compassion is understanding, the ability to recognize the physical, material, and psychological suffering of others, to put ourselves "inside the skin" of the other. We "go inside" their body, feelings, and mental formations, and witness for ourselves their suffering. Shallow observation as an outsider is not enough to see their suffering. We must become one with the subject of our observation. When we are in contact with another's suffering, a feeling of compassion is born in us. Compassion means, literally, 'to suffer with.'"

- Thich Nhat Hanh

The above quote from Thich Nhat Hanh perfectly sums it up: understanding is the foundation, or essence, of love. Living mindfully is very important to cultivating a deeper understanding of the world around us because it's the energy of mindfulness which allows us to see more deeply in our everyday lives. However, you can also take a more "proactive" role to developing understanding. I use a simple exercise regularly that allows me to open up my mind to possibilities and, while it's not necessarily cultivating real understanding, cultivate an environment more conducive to love, compassion, and understanding. I call it *Healing Through Understanding*.

Every day, we're presented with challenges associated when interacting with other people. It's inevitable, there's no way to get around it: when two people come together there's always a chance for conflict to arise. However, each day you also have a choice: to let it go on affecting you in the same way and have it keep causing you stress, anxiety, anger, and resentment or to do something about it.

I know, people tell you to "let it go" all the time, but it's not exactly that easy (you hear it so often- "you gotta' let it go"- that it becomes almost annoying). So, what exactly are you supposed to do? Imagine that the conflict is like someone holding onto your wrist. It's very hard to immediately pull away when someone is holding your wrist, you generally need to turn your hand around in some way that becomes uncomfortable for them so that their grip loosens. From there, you can easily pull away.

Most times when we hold on to things it's very much like this. If you can find a way to change your perspective, to alter your angle, you can see things in a new way. And seeing things in this new way allows you to more easily loosen the "grip" of the thing you're clinging to or which is holding you down. Emotions like anger and resentment are difficult to let go of because we develop the desire to harm others so that we can "get back" at them. However, if we can develop a new perspective, one in which we see the person and the situation more clearly, we'll be able to let go of that anger and resentment and find peace.

I came up with this meditation a long time ago and it's helped me on countless occasions. Sometimes, I call this a compassion or love exercise, and sometimes the understanding exercise, because as I mentioned earlier that's what compassion, as well as love, is all about: understanding.

At the heart of the Healing Through Understanding meditation exists two points:

1. *There's a reason behind every action (we all suffer- we all have challenges and difficulties)*
2. *Everyone is basically good*

When it comes down to it, this exercise is really about working with these two points. Whether it's a friend, loved one, or colleague, the Healing Through Understanding meditation can transform the way you think of another person, help you cultivate compassion and loving-kindness for the person, and in doing so actually help heal the relationship itself as well as the pain you feel in connection with that person.

How to Practice: Healing Through Understanding

Think of someone. This could be someone you hate, someone you generally dislike, or simply a friend or loved one whom you've only recently had an argument or conflict with. Whoever they are, sit and place your focus on this person. Hold the person in your mind as clearly as possible. This, of course, isn't possible in a literal sense, because you don't know everything about the person, but you're holding as much of the person you know- your perception of the person (this is what you've done with the person from the beginning, very important to realize this)- within your mind.

Simply be mindful of the various thoughts and feelings that arise while thinking of this person. Make the effort not to judge anything that arises, simply observe it mindfully. Once you have a decent picture of the person in your mind and you've given it at least three to four minutes to develop while observing mindfully, do these three things:

1. See the picture.

Realize that this very picture in your head, this perception, is what you're drawing judgment based off of. Not off of the real person, but off of your interpretation of that person. This is so important, because most of us make the mistake of assuming that what we see (and what is in our mind) is the way it is. But the reality is, most of the time we only see a fragment of what truly is and what we do see is colored by our bias and prejudices.

2. Contemplate the cause.

Now, think of something which that person does or has done which you disapproved of and think of why they might have done or be doing said thing. If the person said something hurtful to you, start throwing possibilities out there: maybe something is stressing them out and they don't know how to deal with it, maybe they had a tragedy recently or were hurt and don't know how to deal with the anger and sadness they're feeling, or something else. Whatever it is, start thinking of specific possibilities that could be making them act this way. Think of as many as you can.

3. See clearly.

Lastly, take a step back and review these many possibilities which you've brainstormed. Realize that the reason for their hurtful behavior is two things:

1. *Not originating from or because of you, and...*
2. *It's because they suffer in some way.*

In other words, from something which they're experiencing which they don't know how to deal with. Once you've done this, you'll see that there's not just more to the person than meets the eye but that they suffer just like you and I.

To be clear, you don't actually know why they're doing what they're doing. You're simply making an educated guess.

But keeping the two major points in mind, that we all suffer in some way and that we're all basically good, you know that it's something which exists beneath the surface. So, it's by taking the time to brainstorm what that thing might be which is causing suffering for them and leading them to lash out at others that you're able to let go of the anger and resentment within you and transform it into compassion and understanding.

Conflict usually involves one or more people causing harm due to being overcome with frustration from something deep inside of themselves, so if you can realize that the reason this person acted out with anger and aggression wasn't because of you, but because of something deep within themselves that they're hurting from, you can learn to cultivate a great amount of compassion for that person as well as alleviate your own feelings of anger and stress.

This is a very healing exercise which can be done at any time of day and in any situation. We're constantly placed into situations where we have to interact with others, even when just driving on the freeway (and boy is it nice to get cut-off by a dangerous driver with my kids in the car!), so this is an exercise you can use daily to cultivate compassion, loving-kindness, and a deeper understanding of others.

Seeing Love in Others

"To love those that love you is easy. To love those that love you not is not so simple. If you want to change anyone, set a better example. Show more kindness, more understanding, more love. That has a sure effect.

- Yogananda

This Moment

Imagining someone you respect and have a great love for, and practicing seeing them in others is a simple yet extraordinarily powerful meditation. This is very much an active meditation you can use throughout every moment of your daily life and a personal favorite.

This is a short excerpt from a lecture by Ram Dass, the author of *Be Here Now* and it is his response to a question from an audience member on what Maharaji, his teacher (or guru), said about love:

Maharaji on Christ:
"Christ said love all beings as children of God, serve them. Give everything to the poor, even your clothing. Give it all away. Jesus gave it all away including his body.
How did Christ meditate, Maharaji? He was lost in love. He was one with all beings and he had great love for all in the world. He was crucified so that his spirit could spread throughout the world. He was one with God. He sacrificed his body for the dharma. He never died. He never died. He is atman living in the hearts of all. See all beings as the reflection of Christ.
Maharaji, what can I do to gain pure love for Ram? You will get pure love for Ram by the blessings of Christ. Hanuman and Christ are one. They are the same.
What is the best method of meditation? Do as Jesus did and see god in everyone. Take pity on all and love all as God. When Jesus was crucified he felt only love.
Maharaji, who are you? Everyone is a reflection of my face."

If that sounded a bit cryptic, let me offer a more straightforward version of the meditation. Ultimately, for this meditation, you're simply looking deeply into another and seeking to identify those precious universal qualities of love in them.

How to Practice: Seeing Love

1. Choose the object

Depending on your tradition or background, you can choose God, your guru/teacher, or simply someone you have great respect and love for (essentially someone or some thing which represents the highest significance to you).

2. See that person *in* everyone

If your object is someone you respect and love deeply, imagine that *each and every person you meet throughout your day* is that very person. If you respect and love Gandhi, imagine everyone you meet is Gandhi. Imagine how you would treat Gandhi if you were to meet him and treat everyone in this same way. Treat everyone you meet with this deep level of love, compassion, and respect. This significantly changes the way you interact with others.

It's really that simple- but not always so easy. This is a life-long practice which can force you to come face-to-face with hidden bias and attitudes. However, combined with your mindfulness practice to help effectively work through challenges that arise, this is absolutely one of the most powerful meditations I've ever practiced. This practice compliments the practice of mindfulness in another way as well, because to interact with someone in this way is to be fully present for them with all of your being. It's the very definition of mindful presence. Also, to practice Seeing Love requires you keep this practice "to mind", and just as we remember to return to our breath with mindfulness in our mindful breathing practice, it's mindfulness which reminds us to come back to our practice of seeing love when we lose focus.

Following the Path of Love

> *"A new command I give you: Love one another. As I have loved you, so you must love one another. By this all men will know that you are my disciples, if you love one another."*

- Jesus Christ

In this chapter, we covered a number of valuable practices for cultivating qualities such as loving-kindness and compassion. No matter how you decide to bring the qualities of true love into your life, make it an important part of your practice in tandem with the practices of mindful, intentional, and natural living that we've spoken about thus far.

Live the way of love diligently in your everyday life and you'll begin to experience the transformative power of love. A love cultivated from within you, as opposed to a false love that's dependent upon others. Truly, without the cultivation of love, no spiritual practice can be complete. This is, of course, a lifelong effort, but few efforts are as worthy of your time as this. And by walking the path of love both in formal practice and in your everyday life, you'll make progress, one step at a time. As the Buddha said, "drop by drop is the water pot filled. Likewise, the wise man, gathering it little by little, fills himself with good."

Listening & The Great Mirror

"If you love a person, you say to that person, 'Look, I love you, whatever that may be. I've seen quite a bit of it and I know there's lots that I haven't seen, but still it's you and I want you to be what you want to be. And I won't be happy if I've got you in a cage. You'd be a bird without song.'"

- Alan Watts

So far, we've discussed what true love is, the power of that love in the practice of living fully and freely in each moment as well as several meditative practices we can use to begin developing the qualities of true love, particularly loving-kindness and compassion. Now, we'll talk in greater detail about equanimity, which could also be referred to as freedom, and the practice of listening.

To listen is to love. The act of listening itself is an act of nourishing the object which we are listening to. To listen to our bodies is to notice sensations arise and slight changes in the body- a new ache or pain, for instance- and be able to treat it before things get worse. To listen to our mind is to be mindful of what thoughts and feelings arise and to be with our suffering fully in that moment as it unfolds, giving us the ability to heal the wound. And to listen to a loved one is to tend to that love by paying attention to their suffering and being able to provide loving-kindness, compassion, and happiness. To listen is to nurture the quality of that love by deepening one's understanding. In the last chapter, we spoke briefly about understanding as the basis for love. It's listening which allows us to gain understanding, so listening is a key aspect of love in every sense. This is why mindfulness and concentration are often considered the basis for understanding. In mindfulness practice we pay close attention and that act of paying attention is a form of listening. In this way, mindfulness gives us the ability to listen deeply to ourselves and our loved ones.

Listening and understanding coincide with the principle of equanimity, or freedom, which is one of the four principles of true love and something we haven't much touched on yet. Equanimity refers to the ability to allow others to be free and to not cling or attach, therefore clinging is the opposite of equanimity. Unfortunately, more often than not, we cling to an image of what we want our partner to be, what we feel they need to be to fill the void we feel inside. And, in doing so, we clip their wings and take their freedom. This is not equanimity. This is not true love. However, by listening, we can hear the cries of our loved one and see the pain that we're causing them, allowing us to make a change.

Giving Our Loved One Wings

Spontaneity can help us realize the futility in clinging. To act truly spontaneously is to go straight to the heart of things, to act in a way that we're not weighted down by our attachments (natural effort). This is why being spontaneous can feel so good, especially when most else we do is preplanned. A great example of this is in The Hunger Games: Mockingjay, Part I. If you've never watched the movie, sorry, spoiler alert.

This Moment

Near the beginning of the movie, when the rebellion is attempting to rally the various districts together to spur a revolution, Philip Seymour Hoffman and Julliane Moore's characters are attempting to build a set of propaganda videos starring the Mockingjay, Katniss Everdeen (Jennifer Lawrence).

After the first heavily scripted and fabricated attempts at a propaganda video starring Katniss fail, during a meeting reviewing the video Woody Harrelson's character Haymitch stands up and explains how the scripted nature of the video mutes the very fire and spirit which Katniss had become known for and it was only by allowing her to be herself that they would get the rallying propaganda message they were hoping for. Of course, the likelihood of this just happening on its own was next to impossible. For this to happen they needed to place Katniss in a situation that naturally evoked her spirit. Needless to say, the strategy works like a charm.

What does this have to do with anything? The story about Katniss is a classic story about the way we create images in our minds of how another person should behave and then attempt to push those images we've created onto the other person. This is the opposite of equanimity.

We often create unrealistic images in our minds of what we think our spouse should be and how they should act based on a combination of our life experiences and ideas we've been fed or developed. But when they don't live up to those expectations we clash, leading to repeated fights until the point where the tension can hold no further and things finally break. Keep in mind that this doesn't necessarily mean that both people aren't good for each other, but rather that these images they're projecting off onto one another are blocking them from experiencing each other fully as they truly are. This doesn't just show up in intimate relationships, though. This can manifest in parent-child relationships, friendships, and every other type of relationship as well.

This Moment

We project images off on others based on what we're lacking. This is *The Great Mirror*. And when that person doesn't follow through with the image we've projected onto them, a conflict naturally arises.

Examples of specific ideas we tend to cling to are:

- *A husband being chivalrous, when he's really a bit rough around the edges.*
- *A wife being a housekeeper, when she has no desire to be or rather work or own a business.*
- *A wife, husband, or friend fitting in with a certain group of people which their spouse or friend wants to be a part of, when they have very little in common, no desire to build a friendship, and sees that their spouse or friend just wants to feel more important by associating with said group.*

And this can also go in the reverse. In this case, we're building or holding onto relationships which are damaging to us, attempting to convince ourselves they're not bad for us by projecting a positive image of them in our minds:

- *A husband or wife holding onto a positive image of their spouse after they've treated them wrongly and will likely continue to do so ("he/she won't do that again").*
- *A man or woman creating a positive image for someone they desire to be friends with because of some quality they admire but who is really a negative influence ("but they're so cool, I want to learn to be as cool as them").*

Freedom in true love is about accepting someone fully as they are and not forcing some idea about who they should be onto them. To accept someone fully just as they are is in line with the natural flow of life. Not pushing or pulling, not trying to make them something they're not, and not projecting your own issues off on them in an attempt to compensate. This is equanimity. *This* is freedom in true love.

I'll use my relationship with my wife Edith as an example. We have many similarities, but we also have some distinct differences and we don't always agree with each other when it comes to each other's behavior. For this reason, at times in the past we've clashed. However, if I was to project onto her some image of what I think she should be, she'd be a bird without song. It's usually what we try to change in each other or try to project onto each other that have to do with each other's fundamental uniqueness, and so to cut that off would be to cut off the lifeblood that makes the person vibrant and thriving.

To accept her fully, and for her to accept me fully, allows each of us to thrive individually which then results in our relationship together becoming infinitely stronger. This is the power of true love. That is, to accept each other fully without question. However, before we can accept our loved one fully, we must first learn how to listen deeply. It's by listening deeply to our loved one that we can see the messages which this great mirror is showing us. In doing so, we can hear the suffering of our loved one and see clearly that it's us who is projecting our own suffering off on our loved one, therefore making them suffer in return.

When we suffer, without knowing how to skillfully handle that suffering, the first place we look to relieve it is in those closest to us. We argue and yell, take their freedom, and even abuse them verbally. These are all clear signs of the suffering within us, not of any shortcoming of their own. But, without the capacity to listen to the great mirror which reflects our suffering back to us through our loved ones, we won't have the capacity to transform that suffering into peace and freedom. We must learn how to listen deeply to the great mirror with mindfulness and compassion and accept this

This Moment

suffering as our own. By doing this, we can let go of the image we're perpetuating onto our loved one and begin projecting peace and happiness instead. And, when we do this, the great mirror will show us this happiness in return. This isn't always easy and you won't always get it right. But, as long as the effort is there and you live mindfully, you'll be able to listen deeply to yourself and make gradual progress over time.

Take a moment today to think about your closest relationships. Are you projecting some idea about how you want someone to be onto that person? Is someone projecting an image onto you and causing you to feel caged? Is there someone you've been fighting with? That fighting may be coming from these like images we project onto each other. Take a moment to think about the relationships in your life and how this not only might be affecting them but also how you can use this principle of accepting those in your life fully as they are to improve your relationships and your life as a whole.

Lighting up the World with Great Compassion

"Only keep the question, 'What is the best way of helping other people?'"

- Zen master Seung Sahn

In the West, more so than in some parts of the East (particularly Japan), the ego is a stamp of our individuality, without which we believe we'd wither away and become like drones. However, this is a misunderstanding born from the ego itself.

So far, we've spoken about the various aspects of true love, how to cultivate loving-kindness and compassion, discussed the importance of listening and understanding as the foundation of love, and the importance of equanimity, or freedom. But we've left out an important aspect of compassion and perhaps the most significant aspect of the practice of love.

The quality of compassion, *karuna* in the Pali language, is more than just base compassion. The compassion of true love is a compassion which doesn't just feel the suffering of others, it desires to *alleviate* the suffering of others as well. True love isn't just something you feel, it's an altogether opening up of our state of mind to a place where all things are precious and beautiful and equal. And this state compels us to *action*. This coincides with a sort of breaking down of the ego, but that doesn't mean we lose ourselves or our sense of identity, it simply means we gain a clearer understanding. A clearer understanding of our interconnectedness and interbeing nature, as we spoke about in the first chapter of Part IV:

> *In the interbeing of love, I am made up of the suffering of my wife and children. I am also made up of the happiness of my wife and children as well. I am made up of countless non-me elements in each and every moment. This then expands out from us to one other person to all beings at the height of love.*

This is *Great Compassion* and it is the desire to alleviate the suffering of all beings. After the Buddha attained enlightenment, he could have continued living as a hermit, wandering the lands in peace. However, he decided to enter directly into the world and give to all who would listen the wisdom bestowed to him through his deep awakening. For the next forty years after his enlightenment, he continued to travel all across ancient India giving dharma talks and teaching all who would listen.

Zen master Thich Nhat Hanh, author of almost one hundred different titles and the founder of the Order of Interbeing, is someone I deeply respect and a living example of Great Compassion. More than any other person alive today, he has taught me what it means to live in peace and with true love. His entire life is an expression of Great Compassion, from his books, to his numerous monasteries, to his work as a peace advocate, most notably during the Vietnam War, which resulted in his friend Martin Luther King, Jr. to formally nominate him for the Nobel Peace Prize, to the countless dharma talks he's given all around the world for the past several decades. Much like the Buddha, Thich Nhat Hanh has given his life to alleviating the suffering of all beings and to teaching the way of true peace, happiness, and love.

These examples may seem significant, but Great Compassion isn't about being enlightened or writing one hundred books, it's simply about realizing the interbeing nature of all things in each moment and the unifying power of love, thereby being compelled to take action to relieve suffering and create peace and happiness, whether you positively affect one or many.

Light up Your Corner of the World

It is through Great Compassion that the desire to serve is born. This is why it's an integral part of regular Zen practice to serve either (or both) the monastic or surrounding communities in some way. This could include some other form of service for the local community outside the monastery or for the global community at large through volunteering ventures.

It's sometimes misunderstood that Zen monasteries, and the Zen monks and nuns that live and have lived there, close themselves off from society and just practice zazen (literally "sitting meditation" in Japanese) all day long. A core part of many Zen monasteries daily life is daily service in the spirit of mindfulness, love and compassion. This is something you can express in your own life quite easily through countless different ways. The most important way to serve? To carry yourself within the things you already do in your everyday life in a way that expresses these qualities of mindfulness, love, and compassion. To *live the practice*. Practice loving-kindness with strangers and compassion with everyone you meet. And every action you take, be aware of the global community and the way in which we're intrinsically interconnected. In a more outward way, you can take time to serve others through your life's work and in your off-time. This is a big subject that involves big decisions, but just in the way that it's a big decision that shouldn't be taken lightly, your life is a matter of great importance and what you do for 8+ hours a day, or for the hours of off-time you get each week, over the course of your entire life, shouldn't be taken lightly either.

In Buddhist wisdom, it's understood that before you can change the world, you need to change yourself. In fact, to take that further, it's precisely by changing yourself that you can change the world. All you should focus on is lighting up your corner of the world. As you grow, your light will grow. There's no telling how far it will spread. It could simply touch your son or daughter, mother or father, a stranger on the street, or all of the above. It could touch many people or just one. It doesn't matter how many you touch, only that you touch the world with the light of your practice. As you may have noticed, this chapter isn't about a new lesson or meditation practice, it's simply a *call to action.* Living *mindfully, intentionally, naturally,* and with *true love.* Live this practice actively *in your everyday life.* Become the living embodiment of peace, freedom, and true love. The practice which we've outlined throughout *This Moment* naturally cultivates the desire to serve. And it's that service which contributes most heavily to our happiness in life. Live your practice and become an example to others, give your time to those in need, help those who have fallen, show those who have lost their way, and be there for those you love. However you choose to serve, know that it's a two-way street. You're not only serving others; you're serving your own happiness. And by serving yourself in an honest and authentic spiritual sense, through diligently dedicating yourself to your practice, you're serving others as well.

This Moment

The Journey to Yourself

A conclusion to *This Moment.*

Throughout *This Moment*, I outlined an in-depth practice for cultivating greater peace and freedom. We spoke about *living mindfully*, opening ourselves fully to each moment- *One Thing, One Mind, One Moment. Living intentionally* by creating a complete environment which was conducive to those qualities of greater peace and freedom and worked as a container to protect and strengthen our practice of living mindfully, naturally, and lovingly. We spoke about living naturally and learning how to move through this life with greater skill and ease in the face of its greatest challenges. And, finally, we learned how to walk the path of love, learning critical principles to aid in our mindful living practice and cultivating the various qualities of true love not only for ourselves, but also to bring that love to others. Each of the four principles contributed in a unique way to the practice of living fully and freely in each moment of your life.

Throughout *This Moment*, you've walked the journey to yourself. As time went on, "you" began to change in definition and even at times became foggy, but you still arrived at your destination. But, the truth is, you've been at your destination. Each time you sat down to read or listen to *This Moment* was *this moment*. This moment is the only moment. More than anything else, this is the most important point. In each

This Moment

moment, what are you doing? What is going on? Are you being mindful or mindless? Are you being intentional or are you being led astray? Are you being natural or mechanical and conditioned? And are you being loving or critical and closed-minded? This moment is all we've got, so the practice of living fully and freely is the practice of being totally and utterly present for our life in the here and now. Mindfully, intentionally, in harmony, and acting from the deep current of love.

We don't know when will be our last moment. Take what you've learned and apply it diligently, easefully, and joyfully. Delight in the wonder that is the journey to yourself and seek to light up the world with great compassion.

Notes

1. *Being Fully of This Moment, multi-tasking is bad* - business.time.com/2013/04/17/dont-multitask-your-brain-will-thank-you/
2. *Making Mindfulness a Way of Life, 7 Mindful Movements, the dangers of sitting* - mayoclinic.org/healthy-lifestyle/adult-health/expert-answers/sitting/faq-20058005
3. *Making Mindfulness a Way of Life, 7 Mindful Movements, the power of moving mindfully: Louise Hunt of Charted Society of Physiotherapy* - csp.org.uk/frontline/article/moment
4. *Mindful Consumption and the Garden of Consciousness, Eating, eating disorders* - nationaleatingdisorders.org/

About Matt Valentine

Matt Valentine is the founder of Buddhaimonia (Buddhaimonia.com) and a self-published author. He talks weekly on his blog and podcast about mindfulness and meditation practice, rooted in Zen and Buddhist wisdom and practices. He talks about mindfulness & meditation practice, overcoming difficulties, finding peace, letting go, and ultimately how to realize the joyous adventure that life can be. Matt believes that spirituality is simply about coming in touch with our true nature and that by doing so we can discover the greatest gifts that life has to offer.

Matt lives with his wife and three children in Chino Hills, California. You can learn more about Matt at Buddhaimonia.com/about.

More from Matt Valentine

Zen for Everyday Life

Zen for Everyday Life will give you the tools to live every moment of your life mindfully.

Zen for Everyday Life: How to Find Peace and Happiness in the Chaos of Everyday Life is a complete guide to living with mindfulness. In *Zen for Everyday Life*, you'll learn how to mindfully:

- *Walk*
- *Stop*
- *Eat*
- *Drive*
- *Rest*
- *Love*
- *Heal*
- *Communicate*
- *...and much more.*

Zen for Everyday Life will give you the tools to live every moment of your life mindfully and to continue to maintain and nurture your daily mindfulness practice moving forward, guide you through the various myths and misconceptions that keep us from happiness, and show you how to truly deepen your moment-to-moment experience of daily life. You can learn more about *Zen for Everyday Life* by clicking the link below:

Go to <u>ZenforEverydayLife.com</u> to Learn More About Zen for Everyday Life

Buddhaimonia.com

Insight, inspiration, and wisdom for living a more mindful, peaceful, and joy-filled life.

Buddhaimonia.com is the home of Matt's weekly blog, podcast, books, and additional resources. The site's motto is *insight, inspiration, and wisdom for a more mindful, peaceful, and joy-filled life,* and he write weekly about discovering greater peace and happiness through mindfulness and meditative practice.

Matt releases two new articles every week (typically Monday and Tuesday), two new podcast episodes every week (typically Wednesday and Thursday, one of those being a guided meditation episode) and is always working on a new book or resource that will help you live a deeper and more meaningful life. If you'd like to contact Matt, read or listen to additional works, or simply learn more you can visit Buddhaimonia.com or go to one of the specific links below:

Visit Buddhaimonia:

1. Join the newsletter for weekly insight, inspiration, and wisdom: Buddhaimonia.com/newsletter
2. View Matt's Books & Resources: Buddhaimonia.com/books
3. The Buddhaimonia blog: Buddhaimonia.com/blog
4. The Buddhaimonia podcast (on the blog): Buddhaimonia.com/podcast
5. Zen for Everyday Life podcast **on iTunes:** Buddhaimonia.com/iTunes
6. Have a question, request or want to touch base on something? You can contact Matt here: Buddhaimonia.com/contact.

This Moment

This Moment

Distribution

Made in the USA
San Bernardino, CA
30 March 2018